The University of Tennessee Southern

The University of Tennessee Southern

REBIRTH OF AN INSTITUTION

MARK LA BRANCHE AND JENNIFER SICKING

The University of Tennessee

OFFICE OF COMMUNICATIONS AND MARKETING

Contents

Illustrations

Acknowledgments

MARK LA BRANCHE

This amazing and providential story of rebirth required a cast of thousands of committed and mission-driven individuals who made the welfare of the residents of our state an ultimate priority. Without the selfless cooperation and collaboration of trustees, administrators, faculty, students, alumni, legislators, state and local leaders, chambers of commerce and engaged residents, this story could not be told.

This story is a testament to the passion and grit of a small rural college determined to sustain and fulfill its mission and a university system that practices what it preaches in its values statement and takes seriously its role as a land grant university for all Tennesseans.

I would like to express my sincere appreciation to UT System President Randy Boyd for his extraordinary vision, leadership and generosity. He is certainly a hero in this epic story.

So many recognized that this opportunity was an act of God's providence, or what they would refer to as a "God thing." I, too, recognize that providence with gratitude.

Every writer depends on the talents of gifted editors. I owe a debt of gratitude to Emily La Branche Delikat for her editorial assistance in the writing of this book.

JENNIFER SICKING

It's not often that a university adopts another campus, bringing it into its higher education family. Walking with the UT System through its acquisition of Martin Methodist College yielded distinct projects from those we had accomplished in promoting the UT System. This book shares insights about those projects and is, in many ways, a continuation of them.

I am grateful to UT System President Randy Boyd, Vice President of Communications and Marketing Tiffany Carpenter and Assistant Vice President of Communications Melissa Tindell for entrusting me with the opportunity to work on this project. I also appreciate UT Southern Chancellor Emeritus Mark La Branche's patience as I completed my portions. It is also with gratitude that I thank the numerous people interviewed for this book who took time to speak with me and share their thoughts and experiences.

This is a story that will continue to play out in the future generations of students who attend and graduate from UT Southern. It is one without end.

UNIVERSITY OF TENNESSEE SYSTEM
PRESIDENT RANDY BOYD

Serendipity—the art of discovering something truly extraordinary when you least expect it. It's that unanticipated stroke of luck, that chance encounter or that fortunate coincidence that leads us to something wonderful . . . something we were unaware we needed at precisely the right time. Serendipity brought together the University of Tennessee and Martin Methodist College.

It took a collective effort to move a conversation beyond a mere concept to a tangible reality. Both institutions, as well as government and community leaders, banded together to make this acquisition happen. My deepest gratitude to Gov. Bill Lee, the Tennessee General Assembly, our UT Board of Trustees, the Martin Methodist Board of Trustees and the countless stakeholders who supported this historic effort. Their work assures that countless generations will have access to an affordable, public education in Southern Middle Tennessee.

We know that the graduates of Martin Methodist College, and now UT Southern, are vital to the success of that region. The University of Tennessee, as a land grant institution, has a responsibility to provide educational opportunities to the residents of the state. We saw the acquisition as an imperative of our mission. It quickly brought increasing enrollment and retention. The future of UT Southern—and that region—is bright.

In our careers, we make few decisions that will have an enduring impact for others. The acquisition of Martin Methodist College by the University of Tennessee proved to be one and was another step forward in making this the greatest decade in UT's history. It's a decision that will reverberate into the future. History will show that it's even more transformative for that region as future generations of UT Southern's graduates impact and change their communities for many lifetimes to come.

Introduction

This is the story of how a 227-year-old public university system with a statewide presence and a 150-year-old small, rural, church-affiliated college found shared missions and then expanded opportunities to Tennessee's residents. The acquisition, which became effective on July 1, 2021, brought Martin Methodist College, a private college with a public mission in Southern Middle Tennessee, into the University of Tennessee System, a network of campuses and institutes with a public mission to provide access to higher education throughout the state of Tennessee.

The acquisition of Martin Methodist College (MMC) by the University of Tennessee System merged the geography, assets and mission of Martin Methodist with the mission and capacity of Tennessee's flagship system. In 2018, the UT System began a marketing campaign with the slogan, "Everywhere You Look, UT," and lived by that sentiment with the establishment of the University of Tennessee Southern. For the first time in 225 years of statehood, Southern Middle Tennessee had a public university.

This transformation occurred during the greatest health crisis in more than a century—COVID-19. In spite of this challenge, the merger received the undivided support of leaders throughout the state.

It is the hope that this book will also serve as an exemplar for institutions that desire to sustain, enhance, fulfill and expand their missions in an ever-changing world.

CHAPTER I

The Players

THE ACQUISITION OF Martin Methodist College as the fourth undergraduate campus of the University of Tennessee was bold, aspirational and futuristic. The move required unique qualities in administrators, board members and political leaders to bring a bright new future to Southern Middle Tennessee through the mission of higher education. It took people with vision and daring to create change, people with empathy to recognize the plight of many in Southern Middle Tennessee and people with the courage to say "Yes."

It began with the leaders of both institutions who prized their universities' missions over all other considerations.

UNIVERSITY OF TENNESSEE SYSTEM

As the state's oldest and largest four-year public higher education system, the University of Tennessee System has a long lineage of serving the state's residents. From its beginnings as Blount College in Knoxville in 1794 to the formation of the system in 1968 to today, the university's goal has been to send educated graduates out to change the world. In 2020, it consisted of four campuses and two statewide institutes: UT Knoxville, UT Chattanooga, UT Martin, UT Health Science Center, UT Institute of Agriculture and UT Institute for Public Service. With a presence in all of the state's 95 counties, the university impacts Tennessee residents daily.

The president of the UT System oversees the work of each campus and institute as well as statewide initiatives.

As the 26th UT president, Randy Boyd brought his successful business and entrepreneurial skills along with his public service experience, vision and boundless energy to his leadership of the institution. Boyd served as commissioner of the Tennessee Department of Economic and Community Development under Gov. Bill Haslam and was the architect of Tennessee Promise, a last-dollar scholarship program with a mission to increase the state's postsecondary attainment from 32 percent to 55 percent by 2025. Boyd ran for the office of Tennessee governor in 2018, falling short in the Republican primary to Bill Lee. While Lee and Boyd competed in the political arena, their admiration and respect for each other was always evident. This bond set the foundation for them to collaborate as governor of Tennessee and president of the Tennessee's flagship system of higher education.

THE GREATEST DECADE

Boyd created a culture of urgency around what he envisioned as a season of great opportunity for the University of Tennessee System and pronounced his aspiration that 2019 would begin the greatest decade in the 227-year history of UT. This ambition found a force of urgency in the reality that the state was falling behind in the critical area of postsecondary education. A quickly changing and more complex world demands a highly trained and agile workforce. For Boyd, this obligation to equip residents for the opportunities and challenges ahead meant that postsecondary education must be more accessible and affordable across the state.

"The University of Tennessee is charged with being a ladder up for the working class, the middle class all across the state of Tennessee, to engage with the communities, and to make sure that everybody across the state has access to an affordable, great education," Boyd said. "We have that with three great undergraduate campuses in Chattanooga, Martin and Knoxville."

Boyd knew that adding a fourth undergraduate campus with Martin Methodist College would only help UT further its mission.

UNIVERSITY OF TENNESSEE VALUES

The stated values of the University of Tennessee laid the cultural groundwork for transformational outcomes. The values, expressed in the acronym BE ONE UT, are based upon the principle that the whole is greater than the sum of its parts. This phrase would be an animating force in the pursuit of the "greatest decade." The values are:

Bold and Impactful–Serving the state by tackling grand challenges.

Embrace Diversity–Respecting our individual and organizational uniqueness that makes us stronger.

Optimistic and Visionary–Empowering courageous leadership.

Nimble and Innovative–Inspiring creative and transformational action.

Excel in All We Do–Committing to continuous improvement and outstanding performance.

United and Connected–Collaborating internally and externally for greater collective impact.

Transparent and Trusted–Fostering integrity through openness, accountability and stewardship.

The BE ONE UT values served as a driving force in the acquisition of Martin Methodist. The innovative and historic move of adding a fourth undergraduate campus to the University of Tennessee System is a bold demonstration of each of these values.

The board at UT was chaired by John Compton, the former president of PepsiCo, and included, among others, committee chairs Donnie Smith, former CEO of Tyson Foods; Bill Rhodes, the CEO of AutoZone; and Amy Miles, the former CEO of Regal Entertainment Group. Charlie Hatcher, the Tennessee commissioner of agriculture, also served on the board.

MARTIN METHODIST UNIVERSITY

Founded as Martin Female College in 1870, the school was endowed by Thomas Martin, whose $30,000 aimed to fulfill the dream of his daughter, Victoria, who died at 20 years old. In 1908, the school became part of the Tennessee Conference of the Methodist Episcopal Church, South, and changed its name to Martin College. In 1938, it became coeducational. In 1986, Martin College became Martin Methodist College and, in 1993, it became a four-year institution.

In 2017, Mark La Branche joined Martin Methodist College as president. From serving as a pastor, La Branche moved into higher education as director of church relations at Huntingdon College. He left that college in 2009 as senior vice president and chief advancement officer to become president of Louisburg College, where he served until 2017.

"In the Methodist church, we think knowledge is a divine pursuit," La Branche said.

But to continue that divine pursuit and open it to more people in Southern Middle Tennessee, school leadership had to consider moving Martin Methodist College away from the Methodist church and into the University of Tennessee system. The composition of the Martin Board of Trustees included Roy Nix, chancellor emeritus of East Tennessee State University, and Wayne Andrews, Morehead State University president emeritus. Also serving on Martin's board were a number of prominent attorneys, including Tennessee Supreme Court Justice Connie Clark.

"The church is very proud that they've sustained the mission over the past 151 years and that now the mission will have an expanded future that is highly secure," La Branche said. "My willingness to do the hard thing has to do with the fact that we're here for a critical mission, and that is to develop lives."

In addition, the faculty and staff could embrace the BE ONE UT values. This cultural alignment helped Martin Methodist faculty and staff make a relatively seamless transition programmatically and missionally. This alignment also helped ease the large number of changes required in various operational areas in order to migrate from a private to a public institution.

From the moment the merger was conceived to the rebirth of MMC as UT Southern would be 13 months. The myriad approvals and requirements and the unique timelines for each would keep leaders preparing every day of this 13-month period. In the world of higher education, accomplishing a transition of this size and complexity in 13 months is lightning fast.

CHAPTER 2

The Right Time

A CONSEQUENTIAL CUP OF COFFEE

Sometimes a cup of coffee with another person can change everything.

It can a college.

It can a university system.

Perhaps, it can even change a state.

It all depends on the conversation and the willingness to create change.

In March of 2020, after 18 months serving as interim, Randy Boyd was appointed president of the University of Tennessee System by the board of trustees. He immediately made it a priority to visit UT Agricultural Extension agents in all 95 counties. On May 29, 2020, when Boyd planned a stop in Giles County, he also scheduled an early morning coffee meeting with Mark La Branche, president of Martin Methodist College in Pulaski, to discuss higher education in Tennessee.

Boyd and La Branche met on the Martin Methodist College campus in the Trauger Conference Room, which features a portrait of Martin's namesake and founder, Thomas Martin, who kept a watchful eye on the two men as they spoke from his place on the mantel. In May of 2020, the world was entering the throes of the COVID-19 pandemic. Meetings in person were few, and then only with proper physical distancing and facemasks.

Before the meeting, Boyd wondered if UT and Martin

Methodist would have the opportunity to partner on a program or initiative to assist the residents in the area. He also thought that perhaps, years from the meeting, there might be an opportunity to bring MMC into the UT family. Boyd went into the meeting with no expectations beyond possibly partnering on a program.

"As he talked about their desire to serve the region and the people of the area, it sounded so much like the University of Tennessee's mission, which is to serve all of the people of the state of Tennessee, to provide that ladder up for the working class and the middle class to get a better job and a better education," Boyd said of his conversation with La Branche. "The more we talked, the more we realized our missions are the same."

About 30 minutes into the conversation, as the two men discussed the sustainability challenges facing this small, rural, church-related college, La Branche suggested a merger between the two institutions.

"When he shared his idea, which was one that I had thought of a little bit beforehand, but wasn't quite so bold to propose it on the first date, I immediately said, 'Great idea, Mark. Let's pursue this,'" Boyd said.

What Boyd did not know when he scheduled the meeting was that MMC leaders had begun conversations about the college's future. They had even discussed the possibility of finding a partner for a merger.

Robby Shelton, then Martin Methodist's executive vice president and chief operating officer, knew that many small private schools across the nation were struggling and some had closed.

"When you look at the ones that closed over the last 10 or 15 years, they were small enrollments, rural areas, small endowments. We checked about every box," he said.

While finances were tight, MMC received support from the United Methodist Church and generous donors giving unrestricted funds to the college. But Shelton knew the realities.

"We weren't going to close in the next few months or

couple of years, but I couldn't tell you that we would have financial strength in five or 10 years because it had become much more difficult," he said. "We were living on the generosity of a lot of donors and our tuition was very expensive for this region, so we were going to have to really be creative going forward."

Richard Warren, chair of the Martin Methodist College Board of Trustees, agreed.

"We were not flush financially, but we were not challenged," he said. "We were paying our bills."

Byron Trauger, who had served on the Martin Methodist Board since the 1990s and was chair for nine years before Warren, said that the school was not panicking when it decided to discuss possibilities for its future.

"We didn't think that we were on the precipice of financial disaster. We could see the precipice, but we didn't think we were right there," he said. "I felt quite comfortable that we could see the next probably 10 years, certainly five years without any real difficulty, probably 10. Beyond that it was risky."

Leaders of many small schools—public and private—had found themselves in similar situations—or worse—during recent years. Higher Ed Dive website listed three pressures that small higher education schools faced: lowering tuition, stagnating funding and a shrinking pool of high school graduates. The COVID-19 pandemic and its economic hits created further waves in the higher education ocean for leaders to navigate. For some, the waves threatened to sink their ships. According to the website, between 2016 and spring 2023, more than 90 public and private colleges closed or merged. Declining enrollment rose to the top during a review of reasons cited for those actions.

Those factors were very much in the minds of La Branche, Shelton and the Martin Methodist trustees. When the pandemic hit, trustees formed a task force with administrators to consider action plans, should COVID reduce enrollment by 10 percent—or even more. During meetings regarding it, one trustee said, "Tuition-dependent colleges with fewer than a thousand students are just inherently at risk. This COVID thing has highlighted that for us, but that risk is there every day."

MMC leaders knew the college faced the same headwinds as other small private schools. In the fall of 2018, Martin Methodist had 910 students, but it had fallen to 812 in 2020. Without a U-turn, the enrollment slide could begin fueling itself, which could lead to the closure of the 150-year-old institution. In the spring of 2020, its board of trustees and leadership decided to consider partnerships, collaborations and possible mergers to sustain and expand its mission: providing access to education for everyone.

"Over 50 percent of our students are Pell-Grant eligible. Over 50 percent are first-generation college students," La Branche said. "It was critical to sustain this mission."

The idea had been planted that Martin Methodist needed to look for a merger partner. While in the early stages, the trustees wondered about an alliance or merger with another small faith-based institution. They never imagined or dreamed a partner could be found in the University of Tennessee System.

Then Boyd scheduled the coffee meeting with La Branche.

It became clear that an acquisition would enhance and expand the missions of both institutions by bringing the 800-student institution into the 50,000-student University of Tennessee family.

In "The Infinite Game," Simon Sinek writes that people must think about innovation beyond "thinking out of the box" and should work under the assumption that there is no "box" at all. Boyd and La Branche subscribed to Sinek's strategy of innovation. They did not think of merger as a failure or as giving up. Eliminating boundary perceptions allowed the two men to think missionally, to discover opportunity in an unexpected place.

When La Branche told Shelton of his conversation with Boyd, Shelton harbored unvoiced doubts.

"It sounds great, but it's not really ever going to happen," the lifelong UT fan thought. "I just didn't really think that after 150 years we would be acquired by the University of Tennessee."

But that conversation began a clock and work that would tick toward completion for the next year.

La Branche quotes Victor Hugo, who wrote, "Nothing is more powerful than an idea whose time has come." Though he does offer a caveat to Hugo's words: "When that idea hit, well, there's nothing more powerful than a person who's as passionate as Randy."

Merging the two institutions was an idea whose time had come for Martin Methodist, the University of Tennessee and the state of Tennessee. As the leaders began to share the idea, they found it resonating with other people as well. They first presented their vision to UT Board of Trustees Chair John Compton and MMC Board of Trustees Chair Richard Warren. Both wanted to explore it further. Boyd then brought the idea to Gov. Bill Lee and Tennessee Higher Education Commissioner Michael Krause. Boyd knew that the support of these two critical leaders gave the opportunity a much greater chance at becoming reality. With their support, it would experience powerful momentum. Both leaders received the idea with enthusiasm.

La Branche brought the idea to the Tennessee Conference of the United Methodist Church Bishop Bill McAlilly, whose support was essential if this United Methodist institution was to claim a new identity.

"I believe this may be a Godsend," the bishop responded.

Martin Methodist College depended on more than $500,000 in annual funding from the conference. However, the conference faced challenges that threatened this level of funding in the future. The conference also was seeking a more sustainable future through a merger of the Tennessee and Memphis conferences to form the Tennessee-Western Kentucky Conference of the United Methodist Church.

A window of opportunity had opened to assess the possibility of a transformational move, for the University of Tennessee to acquire Martin Methodist College.

On June 5, 2020, Boyd, La Branche, Warren, UT System Chief Financial Officer David Miller and Martin Methodist Board of Trustee and alumnus Roy Nicks met in Nashville at Warren's law office.

The leaders left that meeting eager to explore the acquisition idea. Warren and La Branche divided the list of 26 Martin Methodist College trustees and began conversations with them. The trustees responded to the phone calls with surprise, followed by guarded enthusiasm and many questions. For Martin Methodist trustees, the thought of losing the college's identity weighed heavily, but they were buoyed by the opportunity to preserve, expand and enhance its mission.

"My thoughts were fundamentally positive, but with reservation," Trauger said. "For me, a non-negotiable condition was that the type of students that we had been serving for 150 years would continue to be served."

When Boyd discussed entering into a nonbinding letter of intent during the Sept. 11, 2020, public executive committee meeting, the UT trustees wondered whether the outlay of energy and resources necessary to bring in MMC would be a wise investment. However, they wanted to explore the idea of expanding and fulfilling UT's role as a land grant institution.

"In our two-, four- or six-year term on a board like the University of Tennessee, you're going to get faced with two or three decisions that are really going to make a difference," UT Board Chair John Compton said during one of the board's meetings. "I would put this decision in that camp of potentially having a lasting impact—or not, depending on which way we go."

Warren, who had experience buying and selling businesses in his law practice, knew the public relations aspects of the merger would be critical and that a comprehensive communications plan would be needed to offer guidance. Warren provided the resource to secure a public relations consulting firm through a gift from the Jeanette M. Travis Foundation. Martin Methodist hired the Nashville firm of McNeely, Piggott and Fox to work hand-in-hand with the UT System communications and marketing team. While there were many technical aspects to the merger process, leadership knew that its success relied on comprehensive communication with the many affected constituencies.

ACADEMIC ENDORSEMENT

Martin Methodist faculty and staff support of the merger would be essential. Boyd and La Branche spoke about the opportunity with Linda Martin, UT System vice president of academic affairs and student success, and Judy Cheatham, Martin Methodist College provost.

"This was an opportunity for transformational change and I was excited," Martin said. "I'm a game-on kind of person and I love when it's hard and I love when it's a puzzle and I love thinking about process and how do we do it. But I describe myself as tough-minded and tenderhearted. There was a job to do, but there were people involved, there were emotions, there were relationships."

Judy Cheatham, whose father was one of 12 Methodist ministers in her family and raised the first $1 million for Martin Methodist College, stood on the lawn in the center of campus and listened as La Branche told of his meeting with Boyd.

"Hallelujah, hallelujah," said the Columbia, Tennessee, native who returned to the state in 2015 to be provost at the college.

While she knew state support would lower costs for students and a public institution would help the region with economic and intellectual development, she knew the merger would help solve another dilemma.

"I had trouble attracting faculty because they had never

heard of Martin Methodist," she said. "Just turning into University of Tennessee, I thought, 'Man, this is going to make my recruiting a lot easier.'"

But there would be much to do and many decisions that would need to happen before that could occur.

PRIVATE CONSIDERATION

As a private institution, the Martin Methodist trustees could meet to discuss the opportunity before them without public notice. On Aug. 21, 2020, members of the UT System and MMC administrations and MMC trustees met at Franklin First UMC in Franklin, Tennessee. Boyd, Miller and Martin spoke to them about the UT System, its mission and goals. Encouraged by what they heard from UT System leaders, the MMC trustees, with some caution, decided to move forward.

"We could take our mission statement and lay it right on top of everything you just said," Warren told Boyd during the meeting. "Byron and I both heard somebody who sincerely wanted to help us preserve and expand the constituency that the school traditionally served. That was exactly what we were looking for. Even the people who were most nostalgic about losing the connection to the Methodist church recognized it would just devastate those counties down there if Martin ever closed. We knew, as part of the University of Tennessee System, we could guarantee its future for a long, long time."

Trauger knew that because Martin Methodist was not on the precipice of financial disaster the school could consider the merger from a position of strength.

"That pushed us into what I think was the right frame of mind to say, of these two options, what's the best one for the students we've been serving, for potential students that we haven't been serving who might be served, for the community and for the faculty and the folks who depended on it? What's the best outcome here?"

For UT's leaders, the meeting allowed them to gauge MMC's interest.

"We knew that the only way that the merger would work was if both parties were completely committed to always working toward yes and completion," Miller said. "In something like this, there are many, many ways that are easier not to do it. If you start from a position of skepticism or concern, you can simply question something to death because frankly all the questions you can ask are not solvable."

But that did not mean UT leaders were not going to ask questions and do their due diligence.

STATE OF AFFAIRS

As the UT and MMC leadership teams met privately, their plans would soon dovetail with statewide aspirations.

Longtime business owner Bill Lee had campaigned for governor on the needs of the rural areas of Tennessee. His first executive order focused the attention of state government on strengthening rural areas.

Early in his term, Lee and his cabinet held the first Governor's Rural Opportunity Summit to meet with leaders of distressed counties. In rural areas, one of the keys to economic growth is access to an affordable and quality postsecondary education. When Boyd served as special advisor on higher education under previous Tennessee Gov. Bill Haslam, he designed what became known as the Drive to 55, which launched in 2013. The state of Tennessee set an ambitious goal to see 55 percent of high school graduates receive some form of postsecondary credential by the year 2025 in order to meet industry and business hiring needs. This goal proved a challenge in Southern Middle Tennessee, given the lack of access to a Tennessee public university. Any one of the four public universities across the border in Alabama was more accessible to high school graduates in this area than the public institutions in Tennessee. County and city leaders watched as young people left the area and the state—many not to return—creating a drain of intellectual capital. Many of Tennessee's stars were literally falling on Alabama. Tennessee state leadership wanted a net to catch them.

Finance and timing also played into the state of affairs.

A new public institution would mean additional recurring costs of tuition and building maintenance for the state. However, despite the pandemic, which disrupted and upended economies across the nation, Tennessee found itself in a strong financial position. When the rain fell on the nation and world from the pandemic fallout, Tennessee's financial umbrella held.

Fiscal stewardship put Tennessee in a position other state leaders envied. U.S. News and World Report magazine ranked Tennessee number No. 3 among states in fiscal sustainability, and No. 1 among the 50 states in the category of long-term financial sustainability. In his 2020 State of the State Address, Lee shared that "very few states have minimal debt and a growing rainy-day fund, and this year we propose making an additional $50 million contribution, which is 20 percent more than the statutory requirement."

Even into 2021, as other states continued to struggle, Tennessee found itself in an desirable position.

"A recent report shows Tennessee is one of only seven states to have positive economic growth since April 2020 when much of our economy was shut down. One of seven," Lee said in that year's address. "A strong budget allows us to be good stewards of what the taxpayers have entrusted to us."

A focus on education, a will to improve educational opportunities in rural areas and the financial ability to make it happen swirled together as UT and MMC leaders continued to meet and plan.

CHAPTER 3

Something Brewing

SILENT PHASE

While the idea gained some early momentum, bringing UT and MMC together would require an intentional process. The decision to merge rested in the hands of the boards of the institutions and would require funding by the Tennessee General Assembly. The administrations began gathering the information necessary to drive the decision-making process.

Through the process of researching mergers and acquisitions in higher education, leaders learned that such mergers have been relatively rare during the 20th century. While few books have focused on higher education acquisitions, the leaders found "Strategic Mergers In Higher Education," published by Johns Hopkins Press, which helped guide and confirm the steps. It may have seemed strange to some that Martin Methodist College would seek a merger when it was not in serious peril. However, the authors of "Strategic Mergers" pointed out that the best time to seek a merger is not when it is necessary, but when it is beneficial to advancing the mission of each institution involved. Boyd and La Branche knew that to be the case for the proposal to bring the two institutions together.

Questions, issues and unknowns laid before the leaders in a field that would need to be cleared, tested and prepared for planting before the acquisition could take root. They began by addressing some of the boulders that would need to be removed before the institutions could publicly declare their intent to explore a merger.

SURVEYING THE LANDSCAPE

On July 10, 2020, Senior Vice President and Chief Financial Officer David Miller and UT Executive Director of Capital Projects Austin Oakes landed at Abernathy Field in Pulaski. They joined La Branche, Shelton and Warren in performing a preliminary inspection of the MMC campus and its physical plant. Shelton had prepared a brief report for each facility that included the age of buildings, roofs and HVAC units as well as recent renovations or improvements.

For Shelton, who had harbored doubts about the proposed acquisition, the visit now made the pairing with UT a real possibility. For his part, Warren realized that UT was earnestly contemplating the acquisition.

"When David Miller came over, I realized we were getting serious at that point because Randy is sending the money guy and he was asking all the hard questions," said Warren, who was glad during the inspection that even in the college's financially lean years the board had approved required maintenance.

While a more comprehensive study of the physical plant would occur as a part of the full due diligence, the preliminary inspection assured the UT System representatives that the campus's condition was not likely to be an obstacle to a successful acquisition.

On July 17, 2020, the institutions entered into a mutual nondisclosure agreement to ensure that shared information remained confidential, subject to the requirements of the Tennessee Public Records Act. Then the UT System administration requested MMC's recent financial audits and current financial statements to conduct an initial evaluation of the institution's fiscal state. Martin Methodist had recently completed its 10-year reaffirmation process with the Southern Association of Colleges and School Commission on Colleges

(SACSCOC). In December 2019, the SACSCOC Board of Directors found the college to be in compliance with all the core requirements and standards, and reaffirmed the college's accreditation for 10 years, without any recommendations or monitoring.

PREPARING THE GROUND

Martin Methodist leadership wanted to understand UT's intentions for the acquisition as MMC saw its vulnerability as greater than UT once the proposal became public. A failure to merge could have devastating implications for the small, private, rural college, La Branche said.

Martin Methodist College trustees outlined a series of expectations, terms and conditions during their meeting on Aug. 21, 2020, with which to begin its negotiations with UT:

1. Martin Methodist College will find ways to memorialize its 150-year tradition.
   —Facilities and programs currently named will keep their designation.
   —The Martin name will identify the school of liberal arts (Thomas Martin School of Liberal Arts or Arts and Sciences or Arts and Humanities).
   —The Grissom name will identify the School of Teacher Education (Grissom School of Teacher Education).
2. Employee benefits will increase, including lower health insurance premiums by joining the state insurance system and a greater pension match.
3. Faculty benefits will include increased opportunities for professional development.
4. Being a campus of the UT System will bring a state contribution to offset tuition costs, plant maintenance and capital funds in addition to the state funds to create new academic programs or initiatives as identified through data by economic

development, through the governor's office or
other driving forces. All of this enhancement will
provide a net gain for investment in growth.

5. One-time funds will be requested for the needs
of the transition, including branding, a ramped-up
marketing effort and other "startup" funds as
needed.

6. Shared administrative resources (payroll, enterprise system, purchasing, etc . . .) to accomplish
further efficiencies. UT will provide for transition
to its enterprise system.

7. The UT System will acquire the current debt and
liabilities of the institution, and all MMC assets
will be transferred to the new entity with certain
exceptions to be determined.

8. MMC's academic program will expand dramati-
cally as it taps into the UT's consortium of online
offerings; the academic program can offer additional courses, share faculty and add course offerings with little cost to the institution. In program
areas like business, foreign language and licensure,
this ability will enable students to stay closer to
home in rural areas.

9. MMC's athletic program will continue un-
interrupted. Decisions regarding additions and/
or removal of sports will be made with the
same principles currently employed. Athletic
scholarships will be awarded within the stated
National Association of Intercollegiate Athletic
guidelines.

10. The endowment's mission will be preserved. While
the endowment may be managed with UT assets,
the designations of the endowment will remain
permanently restricted.

11. To ensure a successful transition, trustees
will work to see that the initial board of the
new University of Tennessee campus includes

individuals who understand and are committed to the traditional mission of the institution.

12. MMC will continue to serve Pell-eligible and first-generation students of Southern Middle Tennessee. However, because of increased name recognition in the area and the ability to expand academic programs, MMC should attract more students with average and above average capabilities, allowing STEM programs, including nursing and public health education, to attract better-prepared students.

13. The Associate of Arts and Associate of Science program at MMC will have an opportunity to expand its offerings and should provide a good alternative for the area of the state.

14. Funds and opportunities for staff development and collaboration with the UT System will allow MMC to provide broader and earlier interventions and services to the students it is committed to serve.

15. Student success will find more sustainable support in systemwide collaboration, including a bridge program or something similar to offer students college readiness programs in the summer, before the freshman year.

16. The UT System funding formula is based upon relative increases in retention and graduation rates. The state funding formula for colleges and universities is determined by a trend over a number of years, and MMC will have an option as to when to begin.

18. There will exist autonomy where it makes sense, though initiatives like governmental relations would be more powerful if combined.

19. Tennessee Promise two-year and UT Promise four-year opportunities will extend to the new campus.

20. The Turner Center will remain as an endowed center in collaboration with UT for faith-based

initiatives for the development of thriving rural communities.

21. A Wesley Foundation (Methodist student ministry) will be established.

A PUBLIC DECLARATION

After the two institutions completed the initial phase of due diligence, Boyd and La Branche were ready to make a public declaration of their intent to explore a partnership further. On Sept. 11, 2020, following a discussion at the UT Board of Trustees executive committee meeting, the UT System issued a press release announcing the acquisition exploration and sharing the signed letter of intent approved by both boards. The letter of intent set forth UT's and MMC's commitment to negotiate in good faith to reach an asset transfer agreement to add MMC as a campus of UT pending the conditions set forth and all required approvals.

The terms, built upon the MMC board's expectations, were brief, nonbinding and a starting point for further development and negotiation: "UT and MMC agree to negotiate to affect a potential transfer of all of the assets of MMC to UT." The proposed transaction and negotiations included the following:

- UT will assume certain debt of MMC and MMC will become a financial responsibility of the state of Tennessee.
- MMC will be a new campus of UT and continue to offer a liberal arts experience on a small campus.
- Becoming part of UT will enhance the financial resources available to MMC and its students.
- The current president of MMC will become the chancellor of the new campus.
- UT will retain the existing faculty and staff of MMC as UT employees and will be eligible to

participate in benefits offered by the state of
Tennessee.

- UT will not pay for the transfer of MMC's financial and real estate assets but shall accept financial
  responsibility to continue the MMC campus as a
  going concern and to provide high-quality education to its current and future students.
- The endowment of MMC will be transferred to
  UT and used for the benefit of the MMC campus.
- UT will work with MMC to determine a way to
  honor the mission for the Methodist Church and
  to continue that educational opportunity.

Martin Methodist held four online town hall opportunities
that coincided with the public announcement. Staff, faculty
and alumni would hear of the opportunity and could ask
questions or express thoughts and concerns. The revelation
surprised the different campus communities. Faculty and
staff expressed concerns about how they might be affected.
Anticipating those questions and concerns, the communications teams had developed a question-and-answer document
that was posted on the MMC website that same day. That
document would be expanded as further questions arose. A
microsite, or landing page, was launched to house the latest
sources of information.

With the possibility out in the open, the real work could
begin.

CHAPTER 4

A Deeper Dive

NOW A MORE comprehensive period of due diligence could begin. UT hired Huron Consulting to perform a study and to more deeply examine MMC's finances, programs and operation.

UT also contracted with Bureau Veritas to conduct a formal facility condition assessment. UT leadership wanted to verify the condition of MMC's physical plant to understand if acquiring the facilities would cause any undue burden on the UT System or state.

DUE DILIGENCE—BENEFITS AND RISKS

The complete due diligence study, conducted by Huron, was provided to the UT trustees on Dec. 1, 2020. The report weighed the benefits and risks of the potential acquisition and outlined further considerations. Huron team members wrote, "This report is intended to provide leaders at the UT System and the UT Board of Trustees with sufficient data and analysis to weigh, on the one hand, the benefits of this potential acquisition to Tennessee learners, employers and communities, and, on the other hand, the risks and contingencies of the proposed transaction, such as scaling enrollment and achieving financial sustainability at the new campus."

Huron's analysis of the region, including 19 counties in Southern Middle Tennessee, confirmed a greater need for higher education to meet current and future workforce demands. Data indicated that the college-going rate in the region had decreased and the postsecondary credential rate was low compared to other regions of the state. The Huron team posited that this low rate could be, in part, due to the lack of access to a quality and affordable higher education in the region.

"Few four-year institutions are currently serving the geographic area in and around Giles County, limiting opportunities for students who desire to pursue their education in the region. There is no public four-year institution in the nearly 300-mile distance from Memphis to Chattanooga along the Southern Tennessee border. The nearest private institution is Sewanee, the University of the South, a highly selective university that may be out of reach for some students in the region; the nearest public institution is Middle Tennessee State University, which is approximately 75 miles and 80 minutes northeast of MMC."

Not only are accessible universities scarce in Southern Middle Tennessee, but also four Alabama public institutions situated close to the Tennessee border offer in-state tuition to Tennessee students. More than 1,200 Tennessee high school graduates each year cross the border to attend Alabama public universities that are closer to their homes.

Tennessee and UT leaders have focused on expanding access to college and increasing the number of postsecondary credentials held by its residents through its Drive to 55 efforts, which was led by Boyd during his work for the state. Tennessee Promise, which provides two years of tuition at a community or technical school in the state, and UT Promise, which is a last-dollar scholarship after other financial aid is applied to UT students who qualify, helped to address affordability for Tennessee residents. But the lack of access to a public four-year institution in a significant region of the state created a challenge to this ambitious goal. Filling this gap made the acquisition of Martin Methodist College a high-value target for the state. At the same time, the University of Tennessee System would bring significant value to the mission of Martin Methodist College through its reputation and resources.

While college enrollment has declined at many institutions throughout the state and country, UT has experienced growth in undergraduate students. Huron's analysis showed a clear need for a public campus in Southern Middle Tennessee, and the high-value and probable success of the acquisition in helping the region and state meet their higher education attainment goals.

FINANCIAL ANALYSIS AND ASSUMPTIONS

Huron reported that MMC had assets valued at $35.5 million, with liabilities totaling $9.4 million. Financial statements indicated a drop in net assets in three of the past four years, primarily due to enrollment declines.

Assuming that MMC's line of credit balance would total $1.5 million at the end of fiscal year 2021, Huron estimated that the new campus would need bridge funding from the UT System to address this liability as well as for acquisition and startup expenses. A one-time $1 million funding request was made to the governor and the Tennessee General Assembly for acquisition and startup expenses in addition to the request for $5 million recurring funds needed to offset a 60 percent decrease in the student tuition cost as a state institution.

Based upon its financial projections and assumptions, including assuming the same enrollment as the prior year, Huron estimated that the post-acquisition fiscal year 2022 budget plan would incur a $300,000 operating deficit. Furthermore, Huron's analysis suggested that in order for the new campus to generate positive cash flow for enhancements, contingency needs and sufficient liquidity, enrollment would need to increase by at least 150 students.

FACILITIES—A POSITIVE REPORT

Huron reported in its due diligence study regarding the Martin Methodist facility condition assessment prepared by Bureau Veritas: "Data from Bureau Veritas shows the five-year average facility condition index for universities and colleges they have assessed ranges from 13.01 percent to 20.54 percent with an average of 17.92 percent and the 10-year average ranging from 21.56 percent to 41.63 percent with an average of 29.01 percent. MMC, at 5.8 percent and 15.37 percent respectively, is in comparatively good condition."

The facility condition index measures needed investments to maintain buildings compared to buildings' value. The lower the percentage, the better, explained UT System Assistant Vice President of Capital Projects Austin Oakes, who toured the Martin Methodist campus to evaluate the buildings before the acquisition. The report confirmed the team's initial findings.

"While we had surveyed a limited portion of the facilities at that point in time," he said, "what we saw is that MMC had a history of investing and caring for its facilities. Yes, we would have challenges and it would need renovations and replacements, but the anticipated needs for MMC were not out of line with needs across the UT System. This gave UT confidence that while investment at MMC would be required, these investments were in line with needs common throughout the system."

In an updated report to the UT trustees dated Jan. 15, 2021, Huron included a classroom space analysis based upon enrollment growth targets. The analysis indicated that with 66 percent utilization of classroom space at that time, the institution had room to grow to more than 1,250 full-time students before reaching instructional space capacity.

Huron also provided analysis of campus housing capacity. Using the other UT campuses as a guide, Huron determined that with 30 percent of enrolled students living on campus, the housing capacity could meet the needs of an approximate enrollment of 1,200 full-time students.

These analyses demonstrated that the physical plant had ample space for near-term growth, and the campus could accommodate anticipated enrollment growth for the next five years.

UT FACULTY CONCERNS

During two meetings in October and December, the UT Board of Trustees heard from two UT Knoxville faculty members with concerns about the proposed acquisition.

During the October meeting, Louis Gross, the Alvin and Sally Beaman Distinguished Professor of Ecology and Evolutionary Biology and Mathematics as well as former UT Knoxville faculty senate president, questioned the proposed acquisition, noting that the UT System strategic plan for 2019–2025 made no mention of expansion plans or a process to add new campuses. He posited that UT consider adding units that are already strong contributors to the state's higher education mission, pointing out that Martin Methodist had a low six-year graduation rate of 35 percent while the UT System had a 56 percent six-year graduation rate. He questioned the cost of raising MMC's rate to parity with UT's campuses.

"In sum, prior to further effort on UT System expansion, I suggest that the board request that a deliberate planning process be established, utilizing the professional expertise across the System in higher education, business expansion and state needs, to consider a range of alternatives," he said. "As part of this, I suggest that estimates be made of the resources needed to ensure that any unit added to the System enhances, rather than detracts from, the key strategic goals of the System."

In December, Shawn Spurgeon, UT Knoxville associate professor of counselor education and president of the UT Knoxville faculty senate, spoke to the board. He asked the board to consider the benefit of more analysis and discussion regarding the acquisition.

"Up to this point the involvement of potential university stakeholders appears to have been very limited," he said. "As such, those who would be directly affected by the acquisition, namely faculty and staff, have had limited input and have a minimal awareness of the logistics related to the project. For example, there could be more detailed information and discussion about the potential financial impact of this acquisition on university operations, including the needs of departments and programs."

Spurgeon reminded trustees that people will make assumptions when limited information is available.

"The growth and expansion of the UT System, in my opinion, should be predicated on the notion of open communication and dialogue among stakeholders," he said. "I would like the board to consider deliberate engagement of faculty and staff as stakeholders in this acquisition process."

UT DISCUSSES THE ACQUISITION

When the UT Board of Trustees met virtually during a special meeting on Dec. 9, 2020, Boyd presented the information in the Huron report. As he spoke, he informed trustees that UT wanted to be known for its inclusivity in accepting students, not exclusivity for keeping students out.

"Our land grant mission calls for us to serve all the people of Tennessee," he said. "We are here to provide a ladder up to the working class and middle class, to give them an opportunity for a better education, a better job and a better life."

In acknowledging the report, Boyd said Martin Methodist would be a small acquisition from a financial and student perspective and would not materially change the UT System.

"However, we are not a business looking out for what's in it for us. Instead, we're here to serve the best interests of the people of Tennessee," he said. "As such, this is a part of our state that needs our help and that we absolutely need to serve."

In acknowledging some UT faculty concerns regarding Martin Methodist's academic success, Boyd pointed out it would take work, but the acquisition would be about helping others.

"This is why we signed up for this. This is why we're here—to make a difference. We can change the lives of thousands of young people with a dream for their future and their families who have dreams for them. We can change the future of Southern Middle Tennessee."

UT Board of Trustees Chair John Compton began the discussion, calling the due diligence report on the incipient decline in the area's college-going rate an "eye opener." He said the UT board needed to answer a strategy question of whether UT should have a fourth undergraduate campus and then a tactical question of whether Martin Methodist should be the first step in building a fourth campus.

"When you put the UT brand on this campus, it has to stand for something, and it has to stand for freshman retention. It has to stand for college graduation rates. It has to stand for alumni development. It has to stand for excellence in facilities and safety. It has to stand for diversity," he said. "There's a lot that comes with the UT brand. We just don't put it on something."

Trustee Bill Rhodes acknowledged that he had hesitations about the possible acquisition and that in previous meetings the board hadn't laid out a strategy of wanting to acquire campuses.

"I have no doubt that we can serve the great people of the 19-county region. I have no doubt those individual Tennesseans need to be served as well," he said, adding that growing the student population to a break-even point did not seem to be a good investment of UT finances or intellectual work. "We only have so many people who work in the system. How much of their time has been spent on this already? How much of their time is going to be spent, as you very effectively articulated, to make it the UT brand?"

Rhodes said he supported much about the proposed acquisition, but remained unsure about it.

"If there was a vision like you laid out that it was going to be the size of UT Martin or UT Chattanooga, I'm all in," he said. "If not, a decade from now, it's a 1,200-person campus inside of a 50,000-person enterprise, I don't feel good about that decision."

Boyd said the goal would not be just to grow the potential

new campus by 150 students, but to grow it over time. He pointed out that it took 50 years for UT Chattanooga to grow from 1,000 students to 12,000 students.

"It's our aspiration to grow enrollment significantly, but having a smaller campus within the UT System does provide another alternative for students," Boyd said later in the discussion. "Not every student wants to go to a 7,000-student campus and to have a smaller campus will be appealing to many students. We will expect it to grow, but not being a 5,000- or 10,000-student campus has some merits as well."

UT Trustee Alan Wilson questioned Martin Methodist's outlook, if UT did not acquire it.

Boyd said MMC had lasted for 150 years and proven to be resilient through that time; however, it faced the same challenges as many small colleges.

"There's the possibility that it could fail and then I can't imagine what Southern Middle Tennessee would be without them. They would have nothing, no alternative whatsoever in that part of the state and that would be pretty tragic," Boyd said.

Trustee Kim White asked about the effect on the staff during an already challenging year of the pandemic.

UT System Vice President of Academic Affairs and Student Success Linda Martin acknowledged that the acquisition would require additional work for her staff.

"I think the real value is there are people at Martin Methodist who are passionate about working with us and learning from us and that we wouldn't have to do it all," she said.

UT System Senior Vice President and Chief Financial Officer David Miller said his staff was excited about the opportunity.

"As a system of higher education that is statewide already, we, as the UT System, are uniquely qualified and experienced at adding a campus," he said. "It's a lot of work, but we're going to be working at something. We can just fold this in and keep going. We're actually very energized about it."

Trustee Amy Miles asked if Martin Methodist's academic

programs were suitable for the region and how the programs could impact growth going forward.

"I think it's going to have to be more than just an affordability issue to get to these grander growth plans," she said.

Boyd responded that nursing and teaching had been identified as high-need areas for that region and that conversations had started about possible partnerships. Trustee Donnie Smith said UT needed to think about an agriculture program in that area of the state or a program for students to study two years in Pulaski and then two years at UT Martin or UT Knoxville.

"It would be a great benefit to a very agriculturally abundant part of the state," he said.

After more discussion regarding opportunities and possible issues, UT System General Counsel Ryan Stinnett said the vote that day was to move forward with asking the governor to include funding for the new campus in the budget, requesting the legislature to create a bill approving the acquisition and authorizing UT management to continue negotiations for the asset transfer agreement.

Ultimately, the board approved moving forward with seeking legislative support and continuing negotiations with MMC. However, the UT Board of Trustees requested an additional report from Huron to be shared during the Jan. 22, 2021, executive committee meeting and that it include:

1) Student demographic information for Southern
   Middle Tennessee and the strategy for growing
   the campus;
2) Academic disciplines where the campus can excel;
3) A financial model for the strategy to address
   enrollment, retention and academic success; and
   Plans for engaging stakeholders, including faculty
   and staff, in ongoing discussions regarding the
   proposed acquisition.

"This conversation only pushed the thinking," Compton said at the end of the meeting. "It's really more about how big the opportunity could be and how we're thinking about that. It needs to be thoroughly discussed and debated and analyzed from every possible angle. It will only make us better."

The MMC board also met virtually the same day and approved moving forward with the acquisition.

On Jan. 22, 2021, UT leadership addressed the UT Board of Trustees executive committee, which other trustees also attended, to share the information from the follow-up Huron report.

The report concluded that growing enrollment with traditional college-age students would be challenging as that population was in decline through 2031—the same issue that was affecting much of the country. However, the proposed significant decrease in tuition would likely increase enrollment by more than 3 percent annually. Using UT Martin, located in rural Northwest Tennessee and which serves a similar demographic, as a reference for the retention of students made clear that significant increases in retention were a realistic expectation for MMC with its transition to UT. Huron predicted that through the tuition decrease and a growing focus on retention, the campus could reach 950 students by 2025 and 1,500 students by 2042. With even modest growth in students through enrollment and retention, the campus would break even financially. As enrollment figures would grow, surplus funds could be reinvested in the campus.

"That doesn't take into account the power of the UT brand, which we really can't predict," Martin told trustees in delivering her report on possible enrollment growth during the January meeting. "I would say that it's strongly positive. I think most people in the room would agree, but we can't model that. But I would say that that some of these projections may be very conservative. Also, we weren't able to consider what would happen if we were able to offer tuition breaks to out-of-state students and what that might look like, similar to what's been done at UT Martin or at UT Chattanooga with a great deal of success."

Martin also noted that targeting a growth of 1,500 students would create a unique, small-school environment among the state's public higher education institutions. The state's smallest university at that time was UT Martin, with about 7,000 students. Students preferring a small-school experience would be able to find it—if the proposed acquisition succeeded.

Even the growth of fewer than 100 students would create a positive cash flow for the proposed campus, Miller said. He further explained that the state's financial investment in making it an affordable public education had generated public enthusiasm: "The state is supporting residents with these dollars to provide greater educational opportunity closer to home to make this institution much more affordable."

The report explained that a strategy to grow program offerings was already underway as a result of a Title III Strengthening Institutions Grant awarded to Martin Methodist by the U.S. Department of Education. The grant supported new majors in computer information systems, cybersecurity and public health education. In addition, over the five-year period, the grant would allow MMC to strengthen the technological infrastructure of the institution, modernizing technology in labs and classrooms. The grant would also help track student success and enabled MMC to begin a graduate program in criminal justice and a major in K-12 special education.

Boyd also reported that he participated in town hall meetings and that nearly every city and county in the region as well as government agencies, chambers of commerce, hospitals and one school board passed a resolution to send to the governor in support of the acquisition. "The enthusiasm in the area is incredible," he said. "As we thought before— and as they believe now—that this will be transformative for some of the Middle Tennessee segments." He also reported that conversations with dozens of legislators went well. "This is something that the legislature recognizes is really important for that part of the state and I have strong confidence that they are going to support this initiative, if it's in the governor's budget," he said.

After the report, the acquisition process continued to move forward. Boyd would provide future updates to the board regarding the status of state financial support and other necessary approvals in the process.

"I think each of us probably have gotten more than comfortable with Martin Methodist as we've gone along the way," Compton said to Boyd, Miller and Martin. "One of the facts in the report that really hit home for me was the college-going rate in that part of the state of Tennessee. It's going in the wrong direction and someone has got to step in. As the leader of education across the state, that someone needs to be us. What you all are figuring out is how do we make that happen so that we can meet that need of students and families in that part of the state."

CHAPTER 5

Educating in a New Future

AFTER THE SEPTEMBER 2020 press release announcing UT possibly acquiring Martin Methodist, work of another type began.

Even before the announcement, UT System Vice President of Academic Affairs and Student Success Linda Martin turned her attention to the faculty and programs of the small college.

"I was asked to look at things on the academic side—the quality of faculty, the quality of academic programs," she said. "My biggest concern was academic quality because I really felt like if we wanted our other campuses to respect the faculty and programs at what would be UT Southern, then we had to ensure that they were of high quality. They may not have as many programs. They may not have as many faculty, as many minors or online classes, but it was important that what we did have or what was being offered was of high quality."

Martin worked closely with MMC Provost Judy Cheatham and they decided to move forward with planning as if the acquisition would happen.

"I think we might as well have just shared a house because we were talking all of the time," Martin said with a laugh. The relationship they forged over the months of conversations would be needed later. But for the time, the two leaders worked to prepare Martin Methodist College for a seismic shift.

Martin would review faculty credentials. Cheatham would lead the curriculum and program reviews. Martin Methodist faculty and Cheatham had been discussing revamping their curriculum for five years. "Our gen ed looked like a community college degree, probably because they started off as a two-year degree college and then they turned into a four-year college," Cheatham said.

Needing to put together a plan, Cheatham called Karen Etzkorn (now Galicia), UT System director of academic affairs who worked closely with Martin. As Cheatham listened to Etzkorn, she took notes with her blue ink pen in her blue paper notebooks. One bit of information stood out, all degrees—except engineering—at the University of Tennessee required completion of 120 hours of course credits. At Martin Methodist, degree requirements ranged from 121 hours up to 129 hours.

It was time to revamp the college's entire curriculum.

Shortly after the announcement, Cheatham met with the faculty. She told them that even though the acquisition remained in the possibility phase, they needed to begin working to align MMC's curriculum with UT's. As the curriculum belongs to the faculty, they needed to invest their time into make the necessary cuts and changes.

First to be evaluated were the general education courses that make up the base of all degrees: English, history, math and more. The project MMC faculty had been dreading ended up being one of the easiest. Etzkorn shared with Cheatham the 41 hours of general education courses undergraduate students across the system take. For the faculty and staff at Martin Methodist, with some tweaking, the general education courses fell into place.

From the middle of September 2020 until June 30, 2021, the curriculum committee convened 43 times in meetings lasting up to three hours to discuss every program area and course offered by Martin Methodist. The last meeting was held on the day the UT System Board of Trustees would vote to make the acquisition official.

"I can't say enough about the faculty," Cheatham said. "They were committed to figure out a way to make this better, to make it work."

In the end, the faculty strengthened programs, Cheatham said. Changes in general education requirements lowered the number of prerequisite classes, which allowed the faculty to add classes needed for majors, even while trimming the overall number of credit hours students would complete to graduate as a well-educated adult.

"You have a more cohesive program, and it gives you opportunities," Cheatham said about the changes.

The faculty and staff had to do more than just examine the curriculum. They had to review the course catalog and policies and procedures to make sure they matched those at other campuses in the UT System. As a large, public institution, UT must have policies and procedures that ensure actions are fair and equitable to all. As a small, private institution, Martin Methodist had not recorded many polices, but rather operated from "this is the way we usually do it." Staff members would need to document the guidelines—from how the institution distributed scholarships to how it disciplined students—and make sure they aligned with UT's policies and procedures.

Sarah Catherine Richardson, Martin Methodist dean of students, began attending meetings with other deans from across the system in early 2021. As she listened to conversations, she learned how the campuses handled different issues and about state laws that governed the university's responses to student issues.

"If you ask general counsel, 'Tell me all of the laws that apply to us as the University of Tennessee,' they're like, 'OK, great. Let me send you reams and reams and reams of paper,'" she said with a laugh.

Richardson and her team had to learn and reshape their policies and procedures—from federal Title IX to a state law that requires a notice be sent to parents if a student under 21 has an alcohol violation. But Richardson also received copies of other campuses' procedures as well as help from UT's general counsel office and the other campuses to review Martin Methodist's drafts as the campus prepared for the acquisition.

"I really like a nice organized system and procedure," Richardson said. "You tell me, 'This is the law. We have a system-wide code of conduct; it's been approved by the legislature. This is our policy and then our best practice, which I've confirmed with other campuses, is this procedure.' We treat every student individually and each case is its own case, but for the most, you can kind of rinse and repeat and that frees up all of the emotional energy, that time and all the resources."

Tyler Cox, who served as vice president for enrollment management and assistant athletic director, also had questions when the potential acquisition was announced; he was in the middle of recruiting students for the 2021–2022 school year.

"Who are we recruiting you to? What is the cost? What is our name? There were a lot of unknown questions," he said. "It was very difficult to work through the landscape of what can we say? What can't we say? What color are we wearing? What's our name? What's our mascot? There were just so many unknowns."

He had to prepare to take care of MMC's current students at a private school while recruiting a new class to a potentially public school. He found some students reluctant to commit because of so many unanswered questions. He also had to produce marketing materials discussing the transition and get ready for orientation of a potentially different campus name, colors and mascot.

His preparations came with their concerns: he knew that if the acquisition failed, it could mean the end of Martin Methodist.

"I was telling all who needed to hear it, 'If this falls through, you could cripple us. If we don't make this merger happen, the negative connotations could be the nail in the coffin, unfortunately, for a small private school that put all of our eggs in this basket,'" he said.

Amid all of the uncertainty, Martin traveled to Pulaski to meet with faculty members to answer their questions and assuage their concerns. Martin Methodist faculty members, whose primary obligation is to teach students, wondered if they would need to conduct research and publish papers or books like faculty at UT Knoxville. If they did not, would they be fired? Would they have to teach using UT Knoxville's syllabi? Martin told them they would not face the dreaded "publish or perish" of higher education or follow syllabi for courses taught at UT Knoxville. What the faculty would need to do is scholarly activity, which could occur through research, teaching or outreach.

"I've looked at all of your credentials," Martin told them. "You're doing scholarly outreach."

Martin also encouraged faculty members to contact her with questions or concerns.

"People don't fear change," she said. "They fear what they're going to lose because of the change."

CHAPTER 6

Prospective Phase

ON FEB. 9, 2021, Tennessee Gov. Bill Lee gave his State of the State Address and revealed his proposed budget. His speech marked perhaps the most critical step in the acquisition process.

The Tennessee Higher Education Commission had previously approved UT's request to include $5 million in recurring funding for the new campus in the governor's budget. The recurring funding would replace income due to the 60 percent tuition price drop that would occur once MMC became a part of the state system. UT also requested $1 million in one-time funding to assist with the transition's expenses, which would include legal fees, consulting fees and the rebranding that would be required should the UT System acquire the campus. If the governor had not included the requests in his budget proposal to the legislature, funding the transition would have to be added later as an amendment to the budget, creating a much more difficult path to the acquisition. When Carey Whitworth, UT vice president of government relations and advocacy, relayed that both requests were part of the governor's proposed budget, Boyd and La Branche breathed a deep sigh of relief.

Lee's support of the requests aligned with his promised agenda. The governor had declared in his first order to all executive branch departments that his focus would be on the development of the state's rural counties, noting, "Educational attainment and labor workforce participation are continuing to lag within our rural communities." The absence of a public university in Southern Middle Tennessee's 13 rural counties certainly contributed to this challenge. Four public Alabama universities were located closer to Tennesseans in that region than their own public universities, and each year a significant number of students enrolled at University of North Alabama in Florence, the University of Alabama at Huntsville, Athens State University and Alabama A&M University in Huntsville.

Stakeholders hoped that a public university would not only stem this tide, but also attract students from North Alabama to Tennessee.

Leaving nothing to chance, a full court press began to inform and inspire support in the legislature. The Martin Methodist advancement staff, led by Edna Luna, MMC director of alumni relations, and the UT System Division of Communications and Marketing collected resolutions of support from every county and town in the region and letters of support from business and industry in the region. Whitworth's team delivered them to the legislature.

CHURCH MATTERS

Because the United Methodist Church owned Martin Methodist College, it would be necessary to receive annual conference approval for the merger. The merger would also require the Tennessee Annual Conference Board of Trustees to release the college's assets in its trust, which had been established in 1908. The United Methodist trust clause is a statement included in legal documents declaring that the property and assets of a local church or United Methodist body are held "in trust" for the benefit of the entire denomination. The clause ensures the property will continue to be used for the purposes of the United Methodist Church.

"The Book of Discipline," which sets forth the rules by which the Methodists govern themselves, requires that such a trust clause appear in all deeds of all United Methodist properties. This requirement is a "fundamental expression of

United Methodism whereby local churches and other agencies and institutions within the denomination are both held accountable to and benefit from their connection with the entire worldwide church." "The United Methodist Church Book of Discipline" provides the wording of the trust clause in a variety of forms, depending on whether the property is a place of worship, a parsonage, intended for some other use or acquired from another United Methodist entity.

In December of 2020, the Tennessee Conference trustees approved a release from the trust clause under certain agreed-upon conditions. The resolution would need to be affirmed by conference delegates at the Tennessee-Western Kentucky UMC Annual Conference in June 2021 before the assets of Martin Methodist could formally be released.

The agreed-upon conditions were:

1. The University of Tennessee's commitment to use its best efforts to maintain a college of opportunity in Southern Middle Tennessee similar to what Martin Methodist College has traditionally provided, and to seek to provide additional offerings (such as agricultural and engineering programs) to expand the educational options at the school;

2. The retention and management of the Martin Methodist College endowment by the existing Martin Methodist College nonprofit corporation, or another United Methodist entity acceptable to the Tennessee Conference trustees, such endowment funds to be used in accordance with their designated purposes; and

3. Martin Methodist College's agreement to continue a relationship with the Turner Center, and to retain sufficient real property to continue to provide a location for operation of the Turner Center on or near the campus of the college. The parties agree that the current location of the Turner Center, and the location currently utilized as the residence of

the college president, are both suitable present and/
or future locations for the Turner Center. Should
another location be chosen, Martin Methodist
College shall seek approval of the Tennessee
Annual Conference Board of Trustees, which
approval shall not be unreasonably withheld; and
4. Martin Methodist College's agreement to establish
and maintain a Wesley foundation on or near the
campus of the college, the location of same to
be determined in consultation with the Board of
Higher Education and Campus Ministry of the
Tennessee Annual Conference.

The 2021 Annual Conference of the Tennessee-Western
Kentucky Conference was held virtually June 10–11. Connie
Clark—Tennessee Supreme Court justice, Martin Methodist
College trustee and conference delegate—and La Branche
brought the resolution before the body authorizing a change
in Martin Methodist's conference relationship and the release
of trust. The resolution of the trustees was affirmed with 482
for and 60 against.

ACCREDITATION

The proposed acquisition would need to be approved according to the requirements and standards of the Southern
Association of Colleges and Schools Commission on Colleges
(SACSCOC). This proved a novel situation for the accredi-
tor, in that accreditation does not apply to the University
of Tennessee System as a whole, but to each campus within
it. SACSCOC had to determine whether Martin Methodist
College would retain its accreditation under the ownership
of the University of Tennessee System.

SACSCOC required a six-month notice of intent, which
was satisfied by a formal letter of intent presented to the accrediting body on Sept. 28, 2020. This acquisition of MMC
by the UT System would be classified as a substantive change

request under the category of change of ownership. A substantive change prospectus was due to SACSCOC by March 15, 2021, in order to be considered by the SACSCOC Board of Trustees at its meeting in June. Approval of this request would be necessary for the transfer of assets to occur on July 1. It was a tight schedule, with little room for error.

George Cheatham, Martin Methodist College director of accreditation and institutional effectiveness, led the SACSCOC effort in preparing the proposal. He compiled the data from different departments and worked with the UT System's institutional effectiveness department.

"The UT System did most of the heavy lifting because they had the people in the offices and resources to do it," said Cheatham, who had helped to lead MMC through a successful SACSCOC reaccreditation the previous year.

On June 17, 2021, SACSCOC Vice President and Liaison Denise Young notified the college that the SACSCOC board had approved the request for change of ownership, allowing MMC's accreditation to continue as a UT campus. The SACSCOC board did not list any concerns and were complimentary of the comprehensive process of due diligence and the prospectus as a whole.

A SACSCOC on-site committee visited Nov. 16–17, 2021, to verify that the change of ownership was accomplished within the principles and standards of accreditation as set forth by the organization. The on-site committee completed its work without any findings or recommendations. The SACSCOC board agreed to expedite the decision to give final affirmation to the acquisition at its annual meeting in December 2021. This allowed the college to remain eligible for student aid funding through the U.S. Department of Education Title IV program.

ATTORNEYS AND ATTORNEY GENERAL

Martin Methodist's legal team at the law firm of Sherrard Roe Voigt and Harbison and the legal staff of the UT System navigated myriad legal and contractual elements of the acquisition and merger. Not only was a new institution being formed, but also Martin Methodist College had to be dissolved as a nonprofit organization. The dissolution required the review and approval of the Tennessee attorney general's office. The legal teams assisted in submitting the necessary documents for the dissolution.

UNIVERSITY OF TENNESSEE SYSTEM PRESIDENT RANDY BOYD, LEFT, AND UNIVERSITY OF TENNESSEE SOUTHERN CHANCELLOR MARK LA BRANCHE, RIGHT, WATCH AS MARTIN METHODIST COLLEGE BOARD CHAIR RICHARD WARREN SIGNS DOCUMENTS TO TRANSFER THE ASSETS OF MARTIN METHODIST TO THE UNIVERSITY OF TENNESSEE ON JULY 1, 2021.

UNIVERSITY OF TENNESSEE PRESIDENT RANDY BOYD SPEAKS DURING THE CELEBRATION OF MARTIN METHODIST COLLEGE BECOMING UNIVERSITY OF TENNESSEE SOUTHERN.

TENNESSEE GOV. BILL LEE AND UNIVERSITY OF TENNESSEE
PRESIDENT RANDY BOYD GREET ONE ANOTHER AT THE
CELEBRATION OF MARTIN METHODIST COLLEGE JOINING
THE UNIVERSITY OF TENNESSEE SYSTEM.

TENNESSEE GOV. BILL LEE SPEAKS DURING THE CELEBRATION
MARKING THE TRANSITION OF THE PRIVATE MARTIN
METHODIST COLLEGE TO THE PUBLIC UNIVERSITY OF
TENNESSEE SOUTHERN.

TENNESSEE SPEAKER OF THE HOUSE CAMERON SEXTON, UT
SOUTHERN CHANCELLOR MARK LA BRANCHE, UT SYSTEM
PRESIDENT RANDY BOYD, TENNESSEE GOV. BILL LEE, GILES
COUNTY EXECUTIVE MELISSA GREENE AND PULASKI MAYOR
PAT FORD CUT THE RIBBON TO MARK THE OPENING OF
UNIVERSITY OF TENNESSEE SOUTHERN ON JULY 1, 2021.

UNIVERSITY OF TENNESSEE PRESIDENT RANDY BOYD AND
MARTIN METHODIST COLLEGE PRESIDENT MARK LA BRANCHE
MET ON MAY 29, 2020, FOR A CUP OF COFFEE AND TO
DISCUSS THE STATUS OF HIGHER EDUCATION IN THE STATE
OF TENNESSEE. A PAINTING OF THOMAS MARTIN, WHO
ENDOWED MARTIN FEMALE COLLEGE IN 1870, HANGS IN
THE CONFERENCE ROOM WHERE THE TWO MEN MET.

UNIVERSITY OF TENNESSEE PRESIDENT RANDY BOYD AND
UNIVERSITY OF TENNESSEE SOUTHERN CHANCELLOR MARK
LA BRANCHE STAND BEFORE THE PAINTING OF THOMAS
MARTIN, WHO ENDOWED MARTIN FEMALE COLLEGE IN
1870, BEFORE GRADUATION IN 2022. IT WAS THE FIRST
GRADUATION OF UNIVERSITY OF TENNESSEE SOUTHERN.

CHAPTER 7

Building Momentum and Support

AN IDEA WHOSE time has come creates a force of momentum that breaches resistance and barriers. It also creates energy to cross over each challenge in the process.

Middle Tennessee State University (MTSU) sits about a one-hour drive from the potential new public campus and its administration expressed its opposition in a piece published on Oct. 29, 2020, in the Knoxville News Sentinel. In the article, MTSU President Sidney McPhee shared his concern that the campus would represent a duplication of services and programs. He wrote: "In a time in particular when the state is struggling financially, and also struggling with fully supporting all its universities, adding another separate four-year, public university within 70 miles, one hour, of another major comprehensive university, I really question the economic rationale for that."

The article appeared in the middle of the pandemic—a time when the state economy was in question due to a majority of businesses throughout the state closing shop. MTSU Board of Trustees Chair Stephen Smith also expressed concerns, noting the additional administrative costs would be large: "From a business perspective, rather than adding a new university, with a full set of senior executives and separate academic programs, to the state system, it would make more sense for it to be operated as an extension of an existing entity," Smith remarked in the article. He and McPhee posited that MTSU was well-positioned to add MMC as an extension. UT and MMC continued to work through the acquisition process.

A SOLID FINANCIAL POSITION
AND A GENEROUS CHALLENGE

In early December 2020, the Huron Report issued a financial forecast for the 2021–22 post-acquisition fiscal year: a $300,000 operating deficit after changes from the FY2021 budget of:

1. Reduced net tuition revenue,
2. A $500,000 reduction in church support,
3. Increased salary and benefits expenses,
4. A $4.7 million state appropriation allocation to support operations, and
5. A $500,000 one-time transition support from the state for operating purposes.

Huron also projected that MMC would have a line of credit balance of $1.5 million at the point of acquisition on July 1, 2021. These projections were made on solidly conservative expectations of 2020–21 year-end performance and zero enrollment growth in the first year of acquisition. It presented a possible vulnerability to receiving the necessary support from the Tennessee General Assembly. The assessment also suggested that the financial position post-acquisition would place the new institution in a less than robust financial position.

Boyd responded by challenging La Branche. The Boyd Foundation—launched by Randy Boyd and his family to give to causes including education—would pledge $1 million to the new campus if Martin Methodist could raise $1 million in matching funds. While this proposal demonstrated Boyd's personal belief in the vision, it also allowed other supporters to have "skin in the game," which would be compelling to those who would ultimately make the decisions regarding the acquisition. These dollars would provide a healthy reserve and help allay possible financial concerns by the state legislature, while putting the institution on a firm financial footing.

Inspired by the Boyd family's investment, La Branche saw an opportunity to recognize the first major donors to the new university and to honor the contributions of major figures in the history of each institution. La Branche established the Boyd Family Founders Circle to recognize three levels of support: the Wesley Society, for gifts of $25,000, recognized the college's Methodist roots that had established and sustained it for more than 150 years; the Thomas and Victoria Martin Society, for gifts of $50,000, recognized both the dream of Victoria Martin and the legacy left by Thomas Martin that gave birth to the institution; the Lincoln Society, for gifts of $100,000, recognized President Abraham Lincoln, who signed into law the Land Grant College Act of 1862, or Morrill Act, which provided grants of land to states to finance the establishment of colleges specializing in agriculture and the mechanical arts.

With a list of more than 50 prospective donors identified, La Branche—and often Boyd—began contacting and visiting potential donors. In the five months leading up to the acquisition, gifts surpassed the $1 million challenge, and in the end tallied more than $2 million.

THE IMPORTANCE OF TRUST

In his book "Speed of Trust," Stephen Covey writes that "Change moves at the speed of trust." Trust proved an essential ingredient in building the momentum to successfully complete the acquisition. Some of the terms could not be reduced to a contract with legal obligations. The assurances, particularly the ones that the Martin Methodist Board needed, could only be described as covenantal and relied on the good will and reputation of the parties involved. It required trust. While many aspects could be legally set, others surrounding mission aspects could not. The UT Board members would have to trust the information and data before them and in the vision of the system's administrative leadership. Martin Methodist College required trust that UT would follow through with its intentions and that the endeavor had a high likelihood of success.

Leadership at both institutions also needed to establish trust with the many constituencies within the University of Tennessee System and Martin Methodist College. To do so, the communication teams developed a strategic plan to be transparent and to communicate as much as possible. As part of that, the teams developed the "MMC to UT" microsite, housed on the MMC website, to share the latest information and communication about the process.

Both institutions' leadership took many opportunities to engage various constituencies, listen to their concerns, answer their questions and welcome their advice. With a foundation of trust established at both institutions, people believed in their sincerity and veracity. During the process, when groups expressed that they were not being appropriately engaged, leaders redoubled efforts to include them in discussions.

CHAPTER 8

Preparation for Changes

ON APRIL 29, 2021, the Tennessee Tennessee General Assembly passed the annual budget, which included $6 million in funding for what would be called the University of Tennessee Southern. Though the acquisition cleared that large hurdle, a few more remained.

The Methodist Annual Conference would need to affirm the resolution of the conference trustees releasing Martin Methodist College from the trust clause. The UT System Board of Trustees would need to give final approval to the acquisition during its annual meeting in June.

In preparing to receive approval from the remaining entities, teams at the UT System and Martin Methodist, which had already begun working toward the transition, moved into high gear as they aimed for a seamless transition. "When it's in the governor's budget, it moves from possibility to probability," said Robby Shelton, who oversaw MMC's finances and more as chief operating officer and executive vice president.

The entire MMC staff and faculty would need to go through the hiring and onboarding process to transition to UT and state of Tennessee employees. With Martin Methodist already operating with such a lean staff and faculty, all employees were given the opportunity to stay. But the MMC human resources department had to change over to a new employee system and learn how to operate it and then input Martin Methodist's personnel data. They also had to learn about changes to benefits such as from Martin Methodist's retirement package, which required employees to put in 5 percent of their salaries with the college matching 5 percent, to UT's retirement plan, which also required a 5 percent investment by employees, but the university matched with 9 percent. They also had to arrange insurance and prescription benefit choices to be provided by the state.

At the beginning of 2021, finance team members from both institutions began having weekly meetings—and then up to five or more meetings a week by June—to prepare for the transition. Martin Methodist staff had to be trained in UT banking procedures and business practices as well as new policies that would govern business transactions.

MMC finance team members also had to get ready for students, who would have a much lower cost of attendance. As a state university, the new entity's tuition would be reduced by 60 percent—from $26,000 to about $10,000 per year.

"Most students were going to save thousands and thousands of dollars," Shelton said. "This made the students happy and the parents ecstatic."

But it also meant that MMC staff had to recalculate the cost of attendance and financial aid, including scholarships, for new and returning students.

Information technology had to prepare for domain and website changes as well as for switching MMC's employees over to UT's email system. From student services to finance, the UT System and MMC computer systems would need to be integrated. Staff in each of those areas would need to be trained in UT processes.

New branding to be created for the new UT Southern would have to encapsulate everything from a logo to signage to an athletic mascot.

With a goal for the transition to take place on July 1, 2021, work needed to happen with efficient speed.

CHAPTER 9

Communications and Rebranding

A CONCERTED EFFORT

The partnership between the UT System communications and marketing team, the McNeely, Pigott, and Fox public relations team, and the Martin Methodist leadership team proved integral to the success of the acquisition.

From the beginning, the UT System's communications and marketing team worked from a strategy of transparency to build trust with all of the constituents involved in the acquisition process. From writing press releases for each step in the process to developing plans to promote the merging of the small, private school with the large, public system, the UT team worked with the agency and MMC.

When it became apparent that the acquisition was likely to happen, the public relations and marketing teams went into overdrive. But all of the planning started almost a year before when Boyd and La Branche informed their leadership teams and Martin Methodist hired McNeely, Pigott, and Fox. "I think that was a really good decision because they knew how to roll out a strategy," said MMC Board Chair Richard Warren, who recommended hiring the firm to work on the Martin Methodist side. "They did exactly what we needed for somebody to do. We didn't have anybody else on staff that could have done that."

Weeks before the letter of intent was made public, the teams held several meetings to create a communications strategy for audiences with tactics, key messages and a Q&A

document. The team also managed embargoed interviews with the Tennessean newspaper and the Chronicle of Higher Education, which launched in concert with communications efforts on Sept. 11, 2020, the date the entities announced the exploration of Martin Methodist joining UT. In addition, the teams launched a microsite that would serve to update the public on the progress of the acquisition and included an extensive and growing list of frequently asked questions.

The teams also partnered with Crisp Communications to produce high-quality videos for distribution on social media platforms. The videos featured leaders from Southern Middle Tennessee as well as Martin Methodist students and staff as trusted voices to promote the acquisition. The team's deliberate planning and coordination of messaging and formal communication properly framed what was happening, helped to circumvent misunderstandings and confusion, and allowed leaders of both institutions to speak with one powerful voice.

"Communicating early and being transparent were key objectives of all of the communicators involved," said Tiffany Carpenter, UT System vice president for communications and marketing. "We knew there would be questions and concerns, and we wanted to make sure we had as much information available when the initial announcement was made."

Warren said the public relations plan helped, especially with those concerned about losing the connection to the Methodist church. "They heard the story," he said. "It had been presented in a positive way of what opportunities this was going to create for the school in the future. Frankly, we kept control of the narrative, which is just what you've got to do."

CREATING OWNERSHIP

The institution that was being formed would be Southern Middle Tennessee's university. It was important for the school's surrounding communities to feel a sense of ownership of their university. Faculty, staff, students, parents, alumni and local community members were given opportunities to ask questions and offer input throughout the process. A survey and focus groups with key audiences were conducted during the rebranding process to provide opportunities for MMC's audiences to share their perspectives on what parts of MMC should be maintained, thoughts on a new name for the university as well as the new athletics mascot and colors.

WHAT'S IN A NAME

As confidence grew that the resources and authorizations for the acquisition would be secured, the discussion turned to a name for this potentially fourth undergraduate campus of the University of Tennessee. Through surveys, three names rose in popularity: UT Pulaski, UT South and UT Southern. Each of the other UT undergraduate campuses are named according to their location: UT Knoxville, UT Chattanooga and UT Martin. It was of utmost importance that the entire Southern Middle Tennessee region feel a strong sense of ownership, pride and belonging to the new campus. Because there is the private University of the South in Sewanee, Tennessee, the teams determined that the UT South moniker might cause confusion. Ultimately, the name that garnered the most support would become the name of the reborn institution: University of Tennessee Southern.

Once the name was determined, the UT System marketing team began designing the university brand mark and creating a design guide. Having a plan in place would allow the bookstore to stock new UT Southern gear, and faculty and staff could begin using the new brand marks for meetings, emails and more as soon as the acquisition became official. When it became apparent that the acquisition would move forward, the teams quickly began the work of obtaining new signage for the rebranding of the campus. This swift preparation allowed for a substantial majority of signage throughout campus to display the new brand on July 1, 2021, to coincide with the birth of the University of Tennessee Southern.

A NEW ACADEMIC SEAL

A college seal is the logo that formally represents the institution. It is an official mark used on diplomas, academic honors, university transcripts and formal stationery. With the transition, MMC would need to retire the Martin seal and create a new brand mark. A MMC committee that included officers of the student government association, the faculty council and faculty senate helped design the new seal. Susan Carlisle, MMC graphic artist and director of publications, brought the ideas to life. Through surveys, the team found that the icon and brand element that resonated the most were the campus's historic columns. Including the columns in the design would be a significant way to honor the campus's past as a part of a new seal marking its rebirth. Both the year of MMC's founding, 1870, and the year of its rebirth, 2021, were included on either side of the columns. The Latin phrase in the design—Cognito, Opportunitas and Veritas (Knowledge, Opportunity and Truth)—speaks to the benefits of education and honor MMC's Methodist past.

ATHLETIC BRANDING

Brandie Paul, MMC athletic director and softball coach, had concerns when the acquisition was announced. All of UT's campuses compete athletically in the National Collegiate Athletic Association (NCAA), and Martin Methodist competed in the National Association of Intercollegiate Athletics (NAIA). She wondered if the school would need to change its affiliation to the NCAA or if it would lose its history. Leadership decided that the new school would still compete under NAIA. But with the new name came the opportunity to rebrand Martin Methodist's athletic program.

This would not be the first time Martin had undergone rebranding. Located in the place where two paths of the Trail of Tears intersect, MMC's mascot for many years was the American Indian. In the late 1990s, after a survey of the campus and community, athletics was rebranded as the Redhawks. For more than 20 years, Rowdy the Redhawk served as the campus's mascot.

UT and MMC staff surveyed the community to help determine a new mascot and what current branding elements resonated with them. The results indicated that Tennessee orange was preferred over the color red. Respondents also rated more than 50 proposed team names, including Bobcats, Bucks, Cardinals, Cougars, Coyotes, Eagles, Explorers, Falcons, Flames, Generals, Mavericks, Pacers, Panthers, Pioneers and Redtails. Only two of the proposed team names registered positively: Heat and Firehawk. Leadership opted for Firehawk, as fire would unite MMC's color of red and Redhawk mascot with University of Tennessee orange.

"It keeps our heritage, but it changes it into something new," Paul said.

The various audiences' responses proved vital in the branding transition.

"The community input was integral in the transition. A lot of different audiences have an interest in the success of the campus. By asking for their input along the way, they were able to keep those connections and have stronger buy-in," said Carpenter.

It was important that a new logo design be completed in time to order rebranded uniforms for fall sports. Supply chain issues caused by the pandemic significantly increased the lead time to make this happen. It would also be necessary to rebrand the court in the Curry Athletic Complex along with the signage for the athletic facilities before the teams hit the courts in August. The UT team contracted the services of Danny Wilson, a brand artist, to work with MMC's team to design the new athletic logos, which were completed in June 2021.

CHAPTER 10

Honoring the Past

EVEN AS MARTIN METHODIST faculty and staff prepared for the future, the Martin Methodist College Board of Trustees and leadership began plans to memorialize the school's 151 years of mission. To begin, the founder's legacy would continue at the reborn institution through the Thomas and Victoria Martin School of Arts and Sciences.

Martin Methodist trustees also passed naming resolutions to honor several major contributors in the history of the college. The legacy of Grace Grissom loomed large in the school's history. She served as board chair of Martin Methodist College and built the highly successful business of Mrs. Grissom's Salads. As a philanthropist, she had a special interest in supporting teachers. The trustees passed a resolution to name the School of Teacher Education, the Grissom School of Teacher Education. Recognition of her many contributions are found across campus in the naming of Grissom Natatorium, Grissom Soccer Pitch and Grissom Colonial Hall.

The former Upperman Room in Martin Hall was renamed to honor the Warren-Wilson families, which have a more than 100-year connection to the college. Richard Warren, Martin Methodist board chair, provided leadership during the COVID-19 pandemic and merger with the UT System. He also provided generously to the college through his personal philanthropy and administration of the Jeanette Travis Foundation. His father, Rev. R. Fenton Warren, a distinguished pastor in the Tennessee Conference of the United Methodist

Church, served as a trustee of the college and on staff as director of development. His mother, Katherine Wilson Warren, graduated from Martin College in 1938; his aunt Mildred Wilson Bomar was a member of the 1933 Martin College class, both sent to Martin College during the Great Depression by their father, the Rev. Charles Short Wilson, who was also a minister in the Tennessee Conference.

The Student Life Building was named to honor Jacquelyn "Jackie" Guthrie, who was on the MMC board from 1988 to 2020, serving on and chairing numerous committees. She contributed more than $500,000 to enhance student life spaces on campus. She also endowed three student scholarships in her family's name.

A SERVICE OF REMEMBRANCE AND CELEBRATION

Martin Methodist College Chaplain Laura Kirkpatrick McMasters designed a service of celebration to mark the transition, honor the school's Methodist roots, grieve the loss of identity and lean hopefully into its future as University of Tennessee Southern.

On June 22, 2021, the faculty and staff, including those who had retired, gathered for a meal on the green, to remember the past and share their favorite memories. In front of the iconic columns, attendees sang the "Hymn of Promise:"

> "From the past will come the future
> What it holds, a mystery
> Unrevealed until its season
> Something God alone can see."

Representing the United Methodist Church were Greg Bergquist, general secretary of the General Board of Higher Education and Ministry; Rev. Bill McAlilly, bishop of the Tennessee/Western Kentucky Conference; Rev. Allen Black, district superintendent of the Harpeth River District of the UMC; and Angela Current Felder, chair of the Tennessee/

Western Kentucky Board of Higher Education and Campus Ministry. The Rev. Zach Moffat, pastor of the Pulaski First United Methodist Church and Martin alumnus, brought the message entitled "Carrying the Mantle."

Representing Martin Methodist were La Branche; Warren, Student Government Association President Hayden Galloway; Alumni Board President Brad Butler; Provost Judy Cheatham; Executive Vice President Robby Shelton and McMasters.

Richland Creek, a college bluegrass band entertained, ending its set with a rousing rendition of "Rocky Top," one of 10 official Tennessee state songs, which has become the unofficial UT Knoxville song.

Steve West, faculty emeritus and storyteller extraordinaire, shared humorous tales of academic days gone by. Robby Shelton, a MMC employee for more than 30 years, shared tales of grit and determination from a much more austere past.

As community members lingered over their meal under the shady oaks, they immersed themselves in memories, enjoying the sacred space between what was and what would be. Contemporary theologian Richard Rohr speaks to the majesty and mystery of what he calls this "sacred space" of liminality, "where we are betwixt and between the familiar and the completely unknown. There alone is our old world left behind, while we are not yet sure of the new existence. That's a good space where genuine newness can begin. Get there often and stay as long as you can by whatever means possible. . . . This is the sacred space where the old world is able to fall apart, and a bigger world is revealed."

In just a little over a week, Martin Methodist College would cease to be as it was known. The old world would fall apart. A bigger world would be revealed.

CHAPTER 11

A Day of Decision

ON THE MORNING of June 25, 2021, the University of Tennessee Board of Trustees gathered for its annual meeting, held that year at the University of Tennessee Health Science Center based in Memphis. Two historic items awaited voting. First, trustees needed to review and pass a resolution to approve the transfer of asset agreement and to take ownership of the assets of Martin Methodist College. Second, they needed to affirm MMC President Mark La Branche as the first chancellor of the University of Tennessee Southern.

"We get to make two, maybe three, decisions that really matter in our terms as trustees and I think we'll look back 10 years from today—assuming we make this decision—that that will be a historical decision this board will reach on behalf of the leadership here," UT Board Chair John Compton said in opening the meeting.

Boyd concurred.

"This will be one of the most historic meetings that we've ever had," he said.

Boyd further pronounced that, as the land grant institution for the state of Tennessee, the university is charged with providing a ladder to the working and middle classes.

"We need to live up to our mission," he said. "We need to provide financial access. We also need to provide geographic access. This opportunity will help us do this."

Vice President of Academic Affairs and Student Success Linda Martin shared her team's work with Martin Methodist while Senior Executive Vice President and Chief Financial Officer David Miller spoke regarding Martin Methodist's financial situation and future outlook. Vice President of Communications and Marketing Tiffany Carpenter shared the steps her team had taken to garner community support and develop branding. Then La Branche shared why MMC desired the acquisition.

Ryan Stinnett, UT System general counsel, gave an overview of the agreement for the proposed acquisition as well the approvals still needed from the MMC Board of Trustees and the Tennessee State Building Commission. He explained that the Tennessee General Assembly would need to pass legislation to create a campus advisory board for the new UT Southern, if the UT Board of Trustees approved the acquisition, and add UT Southern (UTS) to Tennessee statutes that affect the other campuses.

Board members then began discussing whether to approve the acquisition.

Compton led off the discussion.

"I think everyone's going to win and certainly the citizens of our state are going to win by having that UT flag planted in Southern Middle Tennessee," he said.

Trustee Donnie Smith, who grew up in Middle Tennessee, said he was not surprised that people were "eat-up excited" to have UT in their backyard.

"I, too, want to commend the enormous effort that's happened over the last year to get us to this point. It's been a yeoman's effort. I appreciate the thoroughness of having as much as you could possibly have in place today in place."

Trustee Bill Rhodes acknowledged that he had expressed concerns about acquiring the school.

"I appreciate the fact that we vetted this in great detail," he said. "What I have found in acquisitions that work or don't work is the biggest issue is if the cultures match. If the cultures match, those people in those organizations will make it work. I have the utmost confidence that you will make this work and make this a great day for the University of Tennessee and all of our constituents."

Trustee Amy Miles said being a UT Promise mentor gave her a better appreciation for what students face and the need to have higher education available nearby.

"What we've been able to do for students in this area with this decision, thank you very much," she said.

Trustee Kim White noted that she had graduated from UT Chattanooga, the system's last acquisition in 1969.

"I will say that becoming part of the system was not just a game changer for the campus, but for our community," she said.

After the discussion by the trustees, the board unanimously approved acquiring Martin Methodist and naming La Branche as its first chancellor. The trustees also passed a resolution approving UT Southern's academic programs, which, they noted, aligned with Tennessee Higher Education Commission policies. They also authorized a bank in Pulaski as a UT Southern depository. The Board of Trustees approved bylaw changes to reflect the addition of the new campus and because UT Southern would continue to be a member of the NAIA.

The Martin Methodist Board of Trustees met immediately following the UT Board of Trustees in a called, virtual meeting to approve the transfer agreement.

"There was some sadness about the loss of the connection to the church, but I think it was outweighed almost in everybody's mind, who shared their views with me, with the opportunity that this provided fidelity to the mission," longtime MMC Trustee Byron Trauger said.

"Frankly everybody on the board loves that college and they want that college to be successful," Richard Warren, MMC board chair said about the vote. "It was just such a compelling case that if you want to guarantee this school's going to be here, we hope for another 150 years, this is the direction we need to go. We can't guarantee that otherwise.

Some people were very sad to see it happen, but I think nearly everybody thinks 'I know this is the right thing to do.'"

With the unanimous approval of both boards, plans could now be completed for the inauguration of the first new public university in the state of Tennessee in more than 50 years. July 1, 2021, would mark the rebirth of an institution.

CHAPTER 12

A New Beginning

LESS THAN A WEEK after the UT Board of Trustees gave final approval to acquiring MMC, a crowd of about 1,500 gathered in downtown Pulaski at 9 p.m. on June 30 to celebrate the change that would arrive at midnight.

Martin Methodist College would live on in the hearts and minds of its faculty and alumni and as the foundation of a new, public institution. The crowd awaited the glow of orange lights that would herald the arrival of the University of Tennessee Southern.

Boyd, La Branche and others joined the crowd to await the momentous occasion. Boyd has often remarked that he considers the 1960s, which included the addition of UT Martin as a stand-alone campus in 1967 and UT Chattanooga in 1969, as the greatest decade in UT's history. He has led the challenge to UT's faculty and staff to make the 2020s even more notable.

"I think the most important way to define our greatest decade is by how we serve the people of the state of Tennessee and by being able to provide new geographic access to a region of our state that was otherwise underserved," he said. "To be able to provide this opportunity for so many people in our state, it will be one of the landmark contributions of this decade."

It had been one year of waiting on the possible threshold of a new life. As the crowd danced to music, the celebration capped the year of work by leaders and teams at both institutions.

"To be in a space where you're letting go of the past, but the future is yet to come, has been suspenseful," La Branche said. "I hate suspense. But now it seems real."

It seemed that way for all who gathered and the excitement that permeated the entire region. The communications teams had worked with the Giles County Chamber of Commerce to prepare for the changeover with yard signs for local businesses and residents, a special section in the local paper and a window painting campaign in the town square. Residents throughout the region prepared to welcome UT Southern.

Now, it came down to a single moment when the clock would tick over.

Boyd led the crowd in the countdown to midnight, chanting down to the birth of UT Southern. At the stroke of midnight, to the cheering crowd, the red floodlights that had lit up the Giles County Courthouse symbolizing MMC's 151-year history turned orange. The University of Tennessee Southern entered the world:

Changing the UT System.

Changing an institution in Southern Middle Tennessee.

Changing, potentially, thousands of lives for generations.

The morning of July 1, 2021, continued the celebration of UT Southern's birth with a VIP breakfast on the green. Gov. Bill Lee and Speaker of the House Cameron Sexton participated in a ceremonial ribbon cutting officially inaugurating the University of Tennessee Southern.

"Our state is better today than it was yesterday because of UT Southern," Lee said.

CHAPTER 13

Turning the Page

WHEN LA BRANCHE was named the first UT Southern chancellor, the assumption was that his leadership would help ensure a smooth and successful transition from Martin Methodist College to UT Southern. With that completed, Boyd and La Branche agreed that the search for UT Southern's long-term leader could be accelerated. On July 1, 2022, La Branche stepped down. Linda Martin, UT System vice president of academic affairs and student success, took over as interim chancellor.

Martin has worked on building relationships—with alumni, donors, faculty and staff, community leaders and other UT campuses. In meetings with donors and community leaders, she tells UT Southern's story. She tells of the missional alignment between the UT System and the former Martin Methodist on caring about students and serving rural communities. She talks about making UT Southern a destination school with students coming from across the U.S. to study and how she wants the school to be defined by a unique student experience. She shares about UT Promise— a last-dollar scholarship that helps qualified students pay for school—as part of her discussion about access and affordability. She also shares about the standard of excellence students find in the faculty there.

With alumni, she lets them know the beating heart of Martin Methodist remains the same and that they have a place at UT Southern.

"If you want to make this successful—any acquisition—
you need to think about that with every communication,
every message, every talk that you give, every interaction that
you have," she said. "If you only talk about the great things
that are happening at UT Southern without acknowledging
the foundation, how it was building on its past, you'll dis-
enfranchise a whole bunch of people really quickly."

In connecting with other campuses, Martin points to the
BE ONE UT values being realized through the nursing program, with the deans from UT Southern and UT Health
Science Center (UTHSC) working to improve the program.
UTHSC performed a full audit of the UT Southern program
and presented a number of recommendations along with
a strategic timeline for implementation. Several of the recommendations were implemented immediately with great
results. In 2020 and 2021, 82 percent of nursing students
passed the national nurse examination. In 2022, 100 percent
of graduating nurses passed. The deans also worked together
to establish a joint Bachelor of Science in Nursing degree
between the two campuses.

Martin also has worked to build relationships between
UT Southern and UT Institute of Agriculture (UTIA). The
campus established an agriculture studies pipeline to prepare
students through 43 hours of coursework before the students would transfer to study at UTIA in Knoxville. UTS also
added agriculture classes, which were not available before,
though the rural area is known for cattle production.

UT Southern also began working with the Tennessee Tree
Improvement Program, based at UTIA. The program planted
a red hickory orchard at UT Southern's East Campus as part
of the program's partnership with Jack Daniels Distillery in
nearby Lynchburg, Tennessee.

"We're just thinking about how to leverage things that
exist across the UT System in a way that we wouldn't have
been able to as Martin Methodist," Martin said.

Martin has worked with faculty and staff to formulate UT
Southern's first strategic plan to guide the campus's priorities
as it moves into the future.

"The campus was extraordinarily willing to change and, for some of them, venturing into the unknown. They really took a leap of faith that still surprises me," Martin said of the faculty and staff's willingness to work through all of the changes of the acquisition and preparation for more to come.

UT Trustee Bill Rhodes praised Martin's efforts.

"We have been blessed by Linda Martin taking on the chancellor role," he said. "She is so talented and passionate."

INTEREST AND ENROLLMENT SOAR

The number of admission inquiries in UT Southern's first two months in 2021 increased by more than 300 percent, and the number of campus visits in the same period increased by more than 900 percent over the previous year.

From an uncertain future, Robby Shelton, then MMC executive vice president and chief financial officer, sees one of promise and potential.

"There's people that live in the next county that's never heard of Martin Methodist College," he said. "People know us now that didn't know us."

The two years following the acquisition, UT Southern has seen its enrollment grow. From 812 students in the fall of 2020, enrollment grew to 876 students in 2021—less than three months after the acquisition had become official. The number of new students in the first class of UTS students increased by 24 percent over the year before. In the fall of 2022, the enrollment grew to 934 students, with a 5.2 percent increase in undergraduate students. Fall 2022 also saw a rise in retention of first-time fall freshmen of more 11 percent. By fall 2023, the student population had grown to 978 students, a 4.7 percent increase from the year before.

Rhodes, who had questioned adding MMC and its enrollment projections, praised the launch of UT Southern.

"Enrollment has climbed into the 900s, but during our deliberations, we defined success as 1,500 or more students," he said. "I look forward to the day when we far exceed that projection."

Others do as well.

"It really beats you down when you're not growing. It really lifts everyone's spirits when you are," Shelton said. "We're going to continue to grow. You don't have to worry about the future of the college five or 10 or 15 or 20 years down the road. I think everybody realizes UT Southern's going to be here long after we're all gone."

The increase in student retention could also be attributed to the increased focus that came with the appointment of a director of student success and the addition of the Pharos 360 student success software management system. Both were made possible by the awarding of a five-year $2.25 million Title III Strengthening Institutions Grant by the U.S. Department of Education in 2020.

"We are in the business of educating our students, retaining our students and graduating our students," Tyler Cox, then associate vice chancellor for admissions and prospective student services, said. "For us to be able to serve this region, it's imperative that we are successful. Our success means our students are successful. That means our region is successful. The University of Tennessee did not bring us into the system to not be successful."

UT Trustee Brad Box sees the future of UT Southern to be one that is brighter than ever.

"I believed it was the right decision when we voted to create UT Southern, but I had no idea that it would create outright celebration in that part of the state," Box said. "The growth in enrollment has also exceeded my expectations. We are going to be able to keep more students in Tennessee with all that UT Southern has to offer and we are going to be able to attract more out-of-state students to Tennessee."

FINANCIALS AND RECORD FUNDRAISING

UT Southern would surpass the expectations outlined in the financial analysis section of the Huron Report. The financial pro forma presented by Huron Consultants in December 2020 predicted a credit line liability upon acquisition of $1.5

million. However, due to close budget management and successful fundraising, the actual credit line balanced zero on July 1, 2021, and the school had a healthy surplus for the 2020–21 fiscal year ahead of the acquisition.

In the first year that UT Southern did not receive the approximately $500,000 in annual support from the United Methodist Conference, the school received annual gifts and pledges totaling an all-time high of almost $5 million. The UT Foundation reported an increase of more than 300 percent in the number of donors to UTS in 2021–22 compared to 2020–21. Evan Beech, who is from Pulaski and who previously served as UTIA's director of advancement, started as a liaison between the UT Foundation and the Martin Methodist fundraising office. He worked to help integrate the two entities through processes and paperwork.

Beech, now the UT Southern vice chancellor of advancement, thinks the possibilities are endless for both the campus and ways to support the faculty and students. He is changing the fundraising strategy from requesting unrestricted dollars to targeted giving toward student scholarships and faculty development endowments.

"I think fundraising, as that department grows, will have several record-setting years," he said. "We need to build our endowment and we're going to do that. We need to keep the public informed, keep our stakeholders informed of all the good we're doing and keep the momentum up."

NATIONAL CHAMPIONS

The athletics program, under the leadership of Athletic Director Brandie Paul, embraced its new brand identity. Facilities and uniforms sported the new colors and Firehawk brand markings while "Flame the Firehawk" entertained as the new mascot. In the first year as the Firehawks, teams brought home two national championships: the women's soccer team won the 2021 NAIA National Championship and the Coed Clay Target Team won the 2021 ACUI National Championship.

HISTORIC MILESTONES

In February 2022, the University of Tennessee Board of Trustees held its winter meeting on the UT Southern campus. In addition to attending to the necessary business of the board, trustees toured the facilities and learned about programs on the newly added undergraduate campus.

On the first evening of the two-day meeting, a banquet celebrated members of the University of Tennessee Southern's Boyd Family Founders Circle, which included unveiling the Founders Wall on the first floor of the Colonial Hall administrative building, once home to Tennessee Gov. Neil Smith Brown.

During the meeting, the UT Board of Trustees approved expanding the footprint of UT Southern's main campus by purchasing two homes contiguous to its existing property. One home directly across from campus was converted into offices to help relieve crowded spaces.

On Feb. 16, 2022, during UT Day on the Hill, the state's House and Senate Education Administration Committees put forth enabling legislation to formally codify the University of Tennessee Southern as an institution of the state of Tennessee. The legislation met unanimous approval in both the house and senate.

A NATURAL PARTNERSHIP

The merger and acquisition process coincided with the completion and opening of the Southern Tennessee Higher Education Center in Lawrenceburg, Tennessee. Located on 40 acres, the center had long been the dream of city and county leadership to establish greater access to higher education in Southern Middle Tennessee. The new home for the Lawrenceburg Branch of Columbia State Community College, the center would also provide community space and an extension for the completion of four-year academic programs. Just 20 minutes west of its main campus, UT Southern immediately set up an office at the center to advise transfer students and now offers graduate classes and teacher licensure classes on-site with plans to expand offerings.

ONWARD INTO THE FUTURE

"UT is a great brand. It's an easy sell," said Richard Warren, former chair of the MMC Board of Trustees. "People in that part of the world know everything about the University of Tennessee and know what a fine institution it is. I think it's only going to get better."

Byron Trauger, who also served on the Martin Methodist Board, agreed about UT Southern's future.

"I'm pleased with the expanded opportunities for students and for faculty. I'm pleased with the reception and the enthusiasm that the whole region, and particularly the Pulaski community and Giles County have given this. I think it's helped invigorate the whole area. While we had pretty high standards with our faculty—and we had some really brilliant faculty members—they have more opportunity now."

UT Trustee Donnie Smith recalled applying to five universities in 1977, but once he received his acceptance letter from UT, he did not open letters from the others. In the fall of 2023, when he spoke during the UT Southern Executive in Residence program, he told students that he knew many in Southern Middle Tennessee felt the same. Though they wanted a UT degree, the dream proved elusive for some.

"Whether it is the need to have a part-time job to help pay for college or the need to commute to school, for many students in Southern Middle Tennessee, the only option was Martin Methodist and it was simply too expensive," he said. "When the University of Tennessee bought Martin Methodist two very important realities flooded into Southern Middle Tennessee. First, there was an affordable option for Tennesseans to get a quality education close to home. That same wonderful phrase that adorns the wall behind my desk, 'the University of Tennessee,' will adorn every diploma conferred by UT Southern. Second, with the UT Promise, providing a last-mile tuition and a good bit of the fees for a student whose family has a household income of less than $75,000, there is no need for any Tennessean to leave Tennessee to get a degree. They can get a degree from our great land grant university, THE University of Tennessee.

"History will look back and confirm that the dawning of UT Southern created an enormous opportunity for hundreds of Tennesseans to create a new trajectory for their lives and families. It takes a bold vision to create this opportunity for so many."

The faculty and staff grow excited when they discuss what is possible for UT Southern.

Sarah Catherine Richardson, the dean of students, said, "We can do something really big here. . . . I don't know a lot about the other systems in other states, but I have drunk the Kool-Aid and it is bright orange. You're going to have to really convince me that anybody else is doing it better than the system. We're able to provide that quality of education in the classroom and outside the classroom, the care, the personal attention in a small town and in a small environment. . . . I think if you're a young person who is looking to be educated, you come from a small town, you don't want to be one in 500, you want people to know your name, you want the best education, you want a really good time, you want to grow as a person and you want to go out and be a leader in your community, this is the place to do it."

The Town's Perspective

PAT FORD

(Includes excerpts from "Our Tennessee" magazine, which is distributed to UT System's donor alumni)

Pat Ford saw he had an email from Martin Methodist College President Mark La Branche asking him to stop by his office to discuss a few things on that summer day in 2020.

It seemed clear that when Ford walked across the campus that La Branche wanted to see him in his mayoral role.

Ford, who graduated from MMC and serves on its faculty, listened in surprise as La Branche told him of the conversations between the college and the University of Tennessee System.

He knew immediately what it could mean for Pulaski, Tennessee, the town he had led since 2010.

"This one single event—this merger—could be the biggest that ever happens in Giles County," he said. "As a leader, it's exciting to be a part of that."

Ford kept the school's secret until the news broke in September 2020. That night, he attended a high school football game.

"I had folks grabbing my arm as I was walking by and asking, 'Is this real talk?'" Ford said.

The Muscle Shoals, Alabama, native has a 30-year history with the college. He planned to attend college in Alabama until he accepted an invitation to visit MMC.

"This is where I want to go to school," he said to his parents about the then two-year college as soon as they stepped out of the car.

He would be among the first graduates in 1996, after it transitioned to a four-year college in 1993.

"I've looked back on it as a turning point in my life," he said of attending MMC. "In high school, I was reserved, quiet and shy. I took a zero on a speech rather than give it."

Ford went to work for the college as an admissions counselor after graduating. He then worked in the athletic department and advancement office. He is currently director of first-year experiences, among other roles. From a student to a staff member, Ford knows the college.

"One hundred percent of what makes it special are the people," he said. "It's family. We support each other; we back each other. There's a caring atmosphere and culture that's been built over the years."

As mayor, he also valued the diverse and highly educated faculty who bring insight from different life experiences to the town of more than 8,000.

"They come from all over the world. They've lived in different places, and you bring them here to a small town," he said. "As the community engages with the college and the college engages with the community, we get to learn different perspectives."

When the acquisition was proposed, community and faculty members shared their thoughts with him.

"I think everybody realized the positive impact it was going to have. With the community, with the faculty, with everybody I talked to, there was just a different vibe," he said. "There was a buzz around town. Everybody was talking about it. Everybody was excited."

Now with UT Southern in Pulaski, Ford foresees good times ahead for the town he led until the end of 2022.

"I think when you start building excitement in your town, that excitement spills over into what industries are looking to locate in a town where people are happy where they live, businesses that want to open up and come to communities that they know is being supportive of new changes, new ideas, new thoughts, new things that are going on," he said.

Because, as Ford said, quoting another faculty member, "Orange brings opportunity."

A Student's Perspective

HAYDEN GALLOWAY

For several reasons, Hayden Galloway chose to enroll at Martin Methodist College (MMC). But she planned to stay only for two years and then transfer.

With their daughter recruited on a soccer scholarship to Martin Methodist, Galloway's parents also encouraged her to remain at home her freshman year. But later she realized something else, she wanted small classes where she would not get lost among the students. She realized big classes and a big campus environment were not for her.

"I would just, quite frankly, maybe be a bit overwhelmed at that," she said. "I wanted something a little bit smaller, especially since I was transitioning out of being homeschooled."

Galloway played soccer, attended classes and participated in the Martin Methodist Student Government Association (SGA).

As she thought about the possibility of transferring to another university for her junior year, one event in her sophomore year changed her mind. An email landed in her inbox announcing that the University of Tennessee System and Martin Methodist College were exploring a merger.

Still, Galloway and the other students had questions.

"We felt like why did UT choose us? We're in Pulaski, Tennessee, which is a very small, rural area. We're a private college. This is unique. This is different. Why were we chosen?" she said.

As about 75 percent of the students also played a sport, they wondered what it would mean for them. Would they have to change conferences? Would they have to play different teams?

But it also created frissons of excitement throughout the campus.

"Because a lot of students are from Tennessee, there was also excitement to attend a UT school. Many students at Martin Methodist chose it because of the student-teacher ratio or because they were local, not because they didn't necessarily want to go to UT Knoxville or UT Chattanooga," Galloway said. "To have the opportunity to be at a UT school, so close to home with tuition that was lowered once we merged, I think brought excitement to a lot of the students."

As the negotiations and discussions progressed through boardrooms and the Tennessee General Assembly, Galloway said MMC faculty answered their questions as best they could. MMC and UT also involved the students in voting on the new emblem, a new mascot and colors for the school.

"I would really like to thank the faculty for letting the students have a say in what our new mascot was and the colors that we kept," she said. "There was a lot of talk on what elements of Martin Methodist were going to be kept when we were UT Southern, and the students and SGA had a say in that."

In Galloway's junior year, she served as president of the now UT Southern's SGA. Even as the students navigated being a public university, Galloway worked to rebuild the government for students after the COVID-19 pandemic.

"Once we became an SGA that was from a UT school, we had opportunities to travel to other UT campuses through networking events, which allowed us to expand on the ideas that we were doing at UT Southern," she said. "Because each campus is so different, it allowed us to bring some different ideas back to our own home campus."

In her senior year, Galloway served as the student trustee on the UT Board of Trustees.

"I realized that this was UT Southern's chance to first make an impression. We're new to the system, and the students that I represented had a lot to say. For the first time, we were able to represent ourselves."

On campus and off, Galloway said the acquisition by UT created more of a sense of community.

"Everyone had UT signs up, everyone was in support of both UT. Online and in-stores, UT merch really became a lot more common," she said. "Not only did UT Southern students have a community feel, but I felt like it kind of impacted the larger community as well."

When she graduated in May 2023, she did so from the University of Tennessee—something she had not anticipated when she enrolled at Martin Methodist.

"Instead of transferring, I felt like my college transferred for me," she said. "So that was kind of awesome to go through."

Letter of Intent from Sept. 11, 2020

LETTER OF INTENT

The University of Tennessee, an instrumentality of the State of Tennessee ("UT"), and Martin Methodist College, a non-profit educational corporation formed under the laws of the State of Tennessee ("MMC"), are discussing the possibility of an agreement for the transfer of the assets of MMC to UT under which MMC would become a part of the UT System, to be governed by the Board of Trustees of UT. This Letter of Intent ("LOI") dated as of September 11, 2020, sets forth UT's and MMC's commitment to negotiate in good faith to reach an asset transfer agreement to add MMC as a campus of UT pending the conditions set forth herein and all required approvals (the "Asset Transfer Agreement"). For purposes of this LOI, UT and MMC may be referred to individual as a "Party" or collectively as the "Parties."

The Parties agree as follows:

1. Intent

UT and MMC agree to negotiate to affect a potential transfer of all of the assets of MMC to UT. Subject to all conditions and required approvals set forth herein, the Parties anticipate that that the proposed transaction may include the following components: UT will assume certain debt of MMC and MMC will become a financial responsibility of the State of

Tennessee. MMC would be a new campus of UT and would continue to offer a liberal arts experience on a small campus. Becoming part of UT would enhance the financial resources available to MMC and its students. The current president of MMC will become the chancellor of the new campus (for purposes of this LOI, such campus is referred to as the "MMC Campus"). UT will retain the existing faculty and staff of MMC as UT employees who shall be eligible to participate in benefits offered by the State of Tennessee. UT will not pay any consideration for the transfer of all of the financial and real estate assets of MMC (the "Asset Transfer") but shall accept financial responsibility to continue the MMC Campus as a going concern and to provide high quality education to its current and future students. The endowment of MMC shall be transferred to UT and shall be designated to be used for the benefit of the MMC campus. UT will work with MMC to determine a way to honor the mission for the Methodist Church and how to continue that educational opportunity, potentially in a partnership with a separate 501(c)(3).

2. Non-Binding Obligation

Notwithstanding anything herein to the contrary, this LOI is non-binding. By executing this LOI and participating in further discussions and conducting due diligence, neither Party assumes any legal or financial obligation to the other Party or any obligation to execute any further agreement, including but not limited to the Asset Transfer Agreement.

3. Approvals

Notwithstanding anything herein to the contrary, the Parties acknowledge and agree that any potential Asset Transfer between the Parties and/ or operation of MMC as a campus of UT, is subject to numerous required approvals, including but not limited to approvals by the following: the governing Boards of both Parties, the Tennessee General Assembly, the Tennessee Higher Education Commission, the Tennessee State School Bond Authority, the Tennessee Attorney General, the U.S. Department of Education, and the Southern Association of Colleges and Schools Commission on Colleges ("SACSCOC"), among other state and federal approving agencies.

4. Nondisclosure

UT and MMC have executed a Mutual Non-Disclosure Agreement dated as of July 17, 2020 and attached as _Exhibit A_ (the "NDA"). The Parties agree that the NDA is enforceable and incorporated by reference into this LOI.

5. Exclusivity

MMC agrees that it will not engage in discussions or negotiations with another institution of higher education or other entity regarding the transfer of its assets during the term of this LOI as set forth below.

6. Due Diligence

The Parties acknowledge that analysis and diligence of each other's information is fundamental to an evaluation of an Asset Transfer. The Parties agree to exchange due diligence requests. Each Party agrees to cooperate in setting up data rooms or otherwise providing the information requested in the respective due diligence lists. Each Party may designate responsive materials as "Confidential" in accordance with the terms of the NDA and this LOI. Each Party shall designate an employee who shall be responsible for gathering and providing due diligence requests to the other Party.

7. Conditions to Close

The Parties agree that the following conditions, among others as may be identified during the term of this LOI, will be conditions to the closing of an Asset Transfer or other similar transaction between the Parties:

Satisfactory due diligence review, creation of
comprehensive list of assets to be transferred,
and evidence that no material adverse change has
occurred.

Negotiation of Asset Transfer Agreement.

Approval of the Boards of UT and MMC.

Approval of the Legislature of the State of Tennessee
and all required State agency approvals, including
but not limited to, the Tennessee Higher Education
Commission and the Tennessee State School Bond
Authority, to the Asset Transfer and operation of
the MMC Campus.

All required Department of Education and other
required federal approvals, particularly approvals
related to accreditation, including SACSCOC, and
participation in federal student loan programs, for
the MMC Campus.

Approval of the Attorney General of the State of
Tennessee to transfer the endowment.

Completion by MMC of the necessary process to
become unaffiliated with the United Methodist
Church.

8. Timeline for Completion of Tasks and Responsible Parties

The Parties agree to use reasonable efforts to complete the
following tasks during the term of this LOI, although they
agree that the failure of either Party to satisfy any component
of the timeline will not constitute a breach of this LOI or
otherwise create any liability to the other Party:

Production of Responsive Due Diligence Materials
Draft of Asset Transfer Agreement
Board Approvals
Legislative Approval
DOE and Accreditation Approval
State Approvals

9. Miscellaneous Provisions

a. *Commencement/Term/Termination.* This LOI takes effect upon the signature of MMC and UT. The LOI will remain in effect until the earlier of (i) the agreement in writing that the Parties will not reach an Asset Transfer Agreement and terminate this LOI or termination by either Party or (ii) one year from the date hereof, unless extended by an executed modification, signed and dated by each Party. This LOI may be modified only through written mutual agreement. This LOI may be terminated at any time by either Party upon thirty (30) days' written notice to the other Party.

b. *Responsibilities of Parties.* Each Party will administer its own activities and utilize its own resources, including the expenditure of its own funds, in performing its obligations under this LOI.

c. *Assignment.* Neither this LOI nor any rights hereunder, in whole or in part, shall be assignable or otherwise transferable without the prior written consent of the other Party.

d. *Not Agents of Each Other.* Nothing contained in this LOI shall be considered to make one Party or any of its employees the agent or employee of another Party.

e. *Publicity Releases.* The Parties agree to coordinate in advance on all public information releases to be issued concerning this LOI. This Section shall not limit either Party in fulfilling its legal obligations to provide information under applicable law.

f. *Counterparts.* This LOI may be executed by the Parties in separate counterparts, each of which, when so executed and delivered, shall be an original, but all counterparts shall together constitute one and the same instrument.

g. *Entire Agreement.* This LOI constitutes the entire agreement between the Parties and supersedes all prior and contemporaneous agreements, understandings, negotiations, and discussions between the Parties, whether oral or written, with respect to an Asset Transfer or establishment of the MMC Campus.

h. *Governing Law.* This Agreement is governed by the laws of the State of Tennessee.

i. *Waiver and Notice.* No waiver of a provision, violation of a provision, or default shall apply to any other provision or subsequent violation or default or be deemed continuous. Any notice, request, approval, or consent required to be given under this LOI will be sufficiently given if in writing and delivered to a Party in person or by recognized overnight courier at the address appearing on the signature page of this LOI under the section titled "Address for notices," or at such other address as each Party may designate in accordance with this LOI. Notice shall be deemed effective upon receipt.

MMC ADDRESS FOR NOTICES:
Dr. Mark La Branche President
Martin Methodist College 433
West Madison Street
Pulaski, Tennessee 38478

UT ADDRESS FOR NOTICES:
David L. Miller, Sr. Vice President
    and Chief Financial Officer
University of Tennessee
709 Andy Holt Tower
Knoxville, Tennessee 37996

MMC POINT OF CONTACT FOR DUE DILIGENCE:
Dr. George Cheatham
Martin Methodist College
433 West Madison Street
Pulaski, Tennessee 38478

UT POINT OF CONTACT FOR DUE DILIGENCE:
C. Ryan Stinnett General Counsel
University of Tennessee
719 Andy Holt Tower
Knoxville, Tennessee 37796

MUTUAL NON-DISCLOSURE AGREEMENT

This Mutual Non-Disclosure Agreement ("Agreement") is entered into and effective as of July 17, 2020 ("Effective Date") by and between the University of Tennessee, a public higher education institution and instrumentality of the State of Tennessee, having offices at 800 Andy Holt Tower, 1331 Circle Park, Knoxville, Teɪmessee 37996 ("UT) and Martin Methodist College, a private institution of higher education, having offices at 433 West Madison Street, Pulaski, TN 38478 ("MMC"). UT and MMC are referred to individually as a "Party" and collectively as the "Parties."

The Parties agree as follows:

1. *Confidential Information.* Each Party possesses proprietary and confidential data, information, documentation, and materials relating to the Purpose (as defined in Section 2). All data, information, documentation, and materials relating to the Purpose disclosed by one Party to the other Party during the term of this Agreement, whether transmitted in writing, orally, electronically, visually, or otherwise, shall be "Confidential Information." The Party receiving Confidential Information is referred to as the "Receiving Party," and the Party

disclosing Confidential Information is referred to
as the "Disclosing Party." All Confidential Information shall be marked with an appropriate restrictive legend, and any Confidential Information
disclosed other than in writing must be reduced to
writing with an appropriate restrictive legend and
delivered to the Receiving Party with.in fifteen (15)
calendar days of the disclosure.

2. *Purpose and Handling of Confidential
Information.* Confidential Information exchanged
between the Parties shall be used solely for
the purpose of discussing a possible merger/
acquisition between the Parties (the "Purpose").
No other use by the Receiving Party of the
Confidential Information is granted without
the written consent of the Disclosing Party. The
Receiving Party shall keep the Disclosing Party's
Confidential Information in strict confidence and
shall not disclose such Confidential Information
to any third party. Other than as permitted in
this Agreement, no Receiving Party may disclose,
modify, copy, transfer, or assign any Confidential
Information disclosed to it under this Agreement.
In the event the Disclosing Party gives its approval
for the Receiving Party to disclose Confidential
Information to a third party, the Receiving Party
shall ensure that all such disclosures are marked
with appropriate legends, the receiving third party
enters into an non-disclosure agreement to protect
Confidential Information with terms at least as
protective as those contained in this Agreement,
and any other conditions reasonably required
by the Disclosing Party in order to preserve the
confidential nature of Uıe information and the
Disclosing Party's rights therein.

3. *Term and Termination.* The term of this Agreement is one (1) year from the Effective Date. The

Agreement may be terminated at any time by either Party upon thirty (30) calendar days' written notice to the other Party.

4. *Obligation Period; Survival of Confidentiality Obligations.* Notwithstanding any expiration or termination of this Agreement, all restrictions and obligations set forth herein, including each Party's confidentiality obligations, shall continue for five (5) years from the Effective Date (the "Obligation Period").

5. *Return of Confidential Information.* Upon expiration or termination of this Agreement or at any time upon written request of the Disclosing Party, the Receiving Party shall promptly return to the Disclosing Party or shall destroy all tangible and digital manifestations of all recorded or stored information that is based on or embodies any of the Confidential Information it received pursuant to this Agreement, except that each Party may retain a total of one (1) copy of such Confidential Information in accordance with its standard archival procedures and in order to determine its obligations under this Agreement.

6. *Ownership of and Rights in Confidential Information; Further Business Relationship.* All Confidential Information remains the property of the Disclosing Party. No license, option, or right is granted to the Receiving Party other than to use the Confidential Information for the Purpose. The Parties are not obligated to enter into any further business relationship or agreement.

7. *Allowed Disclosures of Confidential Information.* UT may disclose Confidential Information to its trustees, officers, and employees (including, but not limited to the UT President's executive leadership team and campus chancellors), and legal and financial advisors who need to know it in

connection with and to accomplish the Purpose. MMC may disclose Confidential Information to its officers, directors, employees, and legal and financial advisors who need to know it in connection with and to accomplish the Purpose, provided such persons are bound by the terms of their employment to comply with this Agreement. Either Party may disclose Confidential Information to the Tennessee Higher Education Commission in connection with and *to* accomplish the Purpose. Additionally, either Party may disclose Confidential Information if required to do so by applicable law, a court order, or a government agency, and if such disclosure is required, that Party shall use reasonable efforts to give the other Party prior written notice.

8. *Exceptions to Confidentiality Obligation.* The restrictions described in this Agreement shall not apply to Confidential Information that:

a. is already lawfully in the Receiving Party's possession at the time of receipt front the Disclosing Party as evidenced by appropriate documentation;

b. is or later becomes public through no fault of the Receiving Party;

c. is at any time developed by or for the Receiving Party independently and without use of or reference to any of the Disclosing Party's Confidential Information disclosed under this Agreement;

d. is lawfully received from a third party whom Receiving Party reasonably believes has the right to make the disclosure, as evidenced by appropriate documentation; or

e. is required by law to be disclosed, including but not limited to the Tennessee Public Records Act, Tenn. Code Ann.§ 10-7-501 et seq.

9. *Governing Law.* This Agreement is governed by the laws of the State of Tennessee, without regard to its conflict of laws principles. Any liability of UT to MMC or third parties for any claims, damages, losses, or costs arising out of or related to acts or omissions by UT, or its trustees, officers, or employees, under this Agreement will be governed by the Tennessee Claims Commission Act, Tenn. Code Ann.§§ 9-8-301 *et seq.*

10. *Entire Agreement; Counterparts; Amendments; Assignment.* This Agreement constitutes the entire understanding between the Parties with regard to the Purpose and supersedes all prior agreements between the Parties with regard to the Purpose. This Agreement may be executed in counterparts, all of which taken together shall constitute one agreement. This Agreement may *only* be amended in writing and must be signed by an authorized representative of each Party. This Agreement may not be assigned, by operation of law or otherwise, or transferred in whole or in part by either Party without the written consent of the other Party.

11. *Waiver.* No waiver of a provision, violation of a provision, or default shall apply to any other provision or subsequent violation or default or be deemed continuous.

12. *Notice.* Any notice, request, approval, or consent required to be given under this Agreement will be sufficiently given if in writing and delivered to a Party in person or by recognized overnight courier at the address provided below. Notice shall be deemed effective upon receipt.

In Their Own Words
Support for the Acquisition

TENNESSEE LT. GOV. RANDY MCNALLY

"The acquisition of Martin Methodist and the establishment of UT Southern was the result of hard work and remarkable vision. When people talk about Tennessee's prosperity and success, quite often they are talking about the Nashville area and other urban and suburban areas. But it is important to remember that there are portions of our state that have not shared that prosperity equally. Much of the reason for that can be traced back to education. The lack of a strong and robust public university presence in Southern Middle Tennessee was hurting the region. The people of Southern Middle Tennessee were clearly being underserved. I am grateful to the University of Tennessee for recognizing that and identifying Martin Methodist as an opportunity. Instead of starting from scratch, the acquisition allows UT to hit the ground running in the region in a way would have been impossible otherwise. Too many young people were either moving out of state or across the state to go to school. This resulted in a brain drain that quite frankly weakened the communities of Southern Middle Tennessee. Before the options for young people in the region were either go away to school or stay put and lose out on opportunities. The establishment of UT Southern gives these bright young people another option. Now they can take advantage of what the UT System has to offer while staying in their community. The social value of this is simply immeasurable."

DR. JOEY HENSLEY: TENNESSEE STATE SENATOR, DISTRICT 28

"This will be a great benefit for all of the citizens of Southern Middle Tennessee and will provide another option for quality, affordable education that will benefit students in this area as well as businesses. I will do all that I can in the legislature to ensure this is successful."

CLAY DOGGETT: TENNESSEE STATE REPRESENTATIVE, DISTRICT 70

"We have the best state college system in the entire nation, and the addition of Martin Methodist College would not only strengthen the entire system but would also enhance the profile of our fine institution and our community."

DR. MARK GREEN: UNITED STATES HOUSE OF REPRESENTATIVES (TN-07)

"A partnership between Martin Methodist College and the University of Tennessee is cause for celebration. Through this partnership, expansive educational opportunities will be available for students in the Southern Middle Tennessee region. This merger will also form a path to retaining rural Tennessee residents after graduation, increasing our educated workforce and recruiting jobs and companies to the Volunteer State's economy. I look forward to watching in the months and years ahead as Martin Methodist College and the University of Tennessee work together to provide educational opportunities for all Tennesseans."

BRADLEY JACKSON: PRESIDENT AND CEO, TENNESSEE CHAMBER OF COMMERCE AND INDUSTRY

"Enhancing Tennessee's skilled workforce is at the core of the Tennessee Chamber's mission. As Tennessee competes for the best jobs, initiatives that can enhance our workforce and give more options for Tennesseans to excel in an in-demand career should be pursued. Collaborations, increased vocational education, specialized skill training, and community driven mergers can all be effective options to achieve our workforce goals. Mergers like the one being proposed will certainly strengthen our communities and result in a healthy business climate that creates economic prosperity for all of Tennessee. The Tennessee Chamber of Commerce and Industry stands ready to take part in conversations about supporting our rural counties through this important partnership between UT and Martin Methodist."

JANET AYERS: PRESIDENT, AYERS FOUNDATION

"We applaud both Martin Methodist College and the University of Tennessee for exploring this merger, and we are excited about the increased opportunities it can bring students, especially in our rural communities along the border of southern Middle Tennessee."

ADAM LISTER: PRESIDENT AND CEO, TENNESSEANS FOR STUDENT SUCCESS

"Every student in every community across the state deserves to be in a classroom with a high-quality teacher. The unfortunate reality in many rural communities across the state, higher education deserts virtually eliminate the likelihood of recruiting these teachers from postsecondary institutions in or near their community. A partnership to incorporate Martin Methodist College as part of the University of Tennessee System will address these critical inequities by ensuring an affordable higher education is accessible for thousands of Tennesseans."

MELISSA GREENE: COUNTY EXECUTIVE & CHAIR OF THE GILES COUNTY COMMISSION

"This proposal would bring much needed growth opportunities to our rural community. But more importantly, this merger will provide untold educational opportunities for the children in the entire south-central Tennessee region."

PAT FORD: PULASKI CITY MAYOR

"This merger is the spark that has been needed to create a dynamic and robust economic and educational footprint in Southern Middle Tennessee. I can only begin to imagine the quality of life it will bring to our community. I wish I could bottle and distribute all the excitement and promise it offers."

VICKIE M. BEARD, DIRECTOR: GILES COUNTY SCHOOL SYSTEM

"This proposal provides a geographically accessible opportunity for affordable post-secondary educational experiences. Additionally, the merger allows for increased early post-secondary opportunities and enhanced career pathways for area high school students."

BRAD BUTLER: GILES COUNTY COMMISSIONER; MMC ALUMNI ASSOCIATION PRESIDENT

"The proposed merger of UT and MMC is an exciting opportunity for Pulaski, Giles County and the surrounding Southern Middle Tennessee area. The expanded educational opportunities UT will provide will make this area even more enticing for prospective students and draw families and businesses that are looking to locate in the area."

JESSIE PARKER: GILES COUNTY CHAMBER OF COMMERCE CEO

"I keep finding myself saying, 'This is perfect.' This merger will expand our quality of life and livability not just in Pulaski, but the region. As a young adult, mother, and citizen, I am overwhelmed with pride for our community and what our future holds. "

RICHARD KELLEY: CHAIR OF THE PULASKI-GILES
ECONOMIC DEVELOPMENT COMMISSION BOARD,
PES & PES ENERGIZE PRESIDENT & CEO

"The proposal would bring new life to our community, offering a broader array of educational and career opportunities. As CEO of PES, chair of the Pulaski-Giles EDC Board and a Rotarian, I stand committed to serving Giles County and striving to build a brighter future for our community. It is my civic duty to support only those projects that are the BEST."

DAVID HAMILTON: EXECUTIVE DIRECTOR,
GILES COUNTY ECONOMIC DEVELOPMENT
COMMISSION

"This proposal will open up many opportunities for our citizens to receive a great education and provide our local businesses and industries with employees prepared to compete in a global economy. The support and quality education offered by UT will provide highly qualified individuals to work with industry and business throughout Southern Middle Tennessee."

JIM EDMONDSON: CEO, SOUTHERN TENNESSEE
REGIONAL HEALTH SYSTEM—PULASKI

"I believe the Martin Methodist College proposed merger with the University of Tennessee will be very good for our regional health care industry. The need for more health care professionals is nearly limitless. Expanding the number of disciplines being taught locally is of high importance but so is the expansion of existing programs like the nursing program. Expansion not only in numbers of students but also, disciplines that can be pursued within the nursing degree."

D. DORAN JOHNSON: SENIOR VICE PRESIDENT, NHC SOUTH CENTRAL REGION

"I have worked in South Central Tennessee my entire career with seniors. The nursing program at MMC has been a great addition for this population. For the senior care industry, daily long-term care such as hospice, home health, rehab services, assisted living and skilled nursing has to be provided close to home so family and loved ones are able to provide psychosocial support. Therefore, the UT and MMC merger will create a process for sustainable future for the development and education of the health care professionals that will serve the rural areas of South Central, Tennessee. This merger will strengthen and greatly contribute to the environmental, social and economic systems of the senior care industry. It will improve the quantity of the health care professionals, adding availability to the interest of our youth. It will undoubtedly improve the quality and quantity of nurses for our seniors. MMC and I have dreamed and studied the possibly, (my dream) of more allied health professionals. If students are supported by the UT System locally, they will be more likely to join the UT allied health programs throughout the state."

BLAKE LAY: LAWRENCEBURG MAYOR

"Having Martin Methodist College become the fourth campus in the UT System will be transformational for the Southern Middle Tennessee region from an educational and economic development perspective. The opportunities UT will provide on every front for this rural area are limitless."

T. R. WILLIAMS: LAWRENCE COUNTY EXECUTIVE

"Thousands of Southern Middle Tennessee students cross the Alabama border to go to college every year because we don't have the educational opportunities they are seeking here at home. This proposal reduces that 'brain drain' and gives our students the opportunity for an education from one of the top public universities in the country."

MICHAEL ADKINS: DIRECTOR OF LAWRENCE COUNTY SCHOOLS

"Partnering MMC's stellar reputation in this region with UT's mission and vision will open doors of opportunity for our students to reach their goals."

RYAN EGLY: PRESIDENT & CEO OF THE LAWRENCE COUNTY CHAMBER

"Access to higher education is the first step of increasing educational attainment and increasing educational attainment in our community is the key to sustaining economic development. For this reason, the University of Tennessee's proposal to acquire Martin Methodist College is not only popular regionally, but is necessary to provide our students with access to a public, four-year institution for the very first time."

GREG LOWE, DIRECTOR OF ECONOMIC DEVELOPMENT, CITY OF LEWISBURG

"Martin Methodist has served our region very well for a century and a half; but the opportunity for it to become a University of Tennessee campus will spur significant growth in the region and workforce and community development. Innovation in the region just leaped forward in 2020."

CHAZ MOLDER: COLUMBIA MAYOR

"We are thrilled to learn of the UT and Martin Methodist College merger as it will join together two well respected institutions which have long played a role in producing job-ready and life-ready graduates. The result of this merger will lead to increased educational opportunities, and a more robust economy in the south-central Tennessee region."

CAROLYN DENTON: EXECUTIVE DIRECTOR, FAYETTEVILLE-LINCOLN COUNTY CHAMBER OF COMMERCE

"This merger would offer more educational opportunities for our students in the region and open doors for economic development and growth. Such exciting news!"

Excerpts of Minutes from June 25, 2021

THE MINUTES OF the University of Tennessee Board meeting on June 25, 2021, contain an important narrative of this historic day. The following excerpts include remarks and actions by the UT System Board Chair John Compton, UT System President Randy Boyd; and President of Martin Methodist College/Inaugural Chancellor of the University of Tennessee Southern Mark La Branche.

UNIVERSITY OF TENNESSEE
BOARD OF TRUSTEES
MINUTES OF THE ANNUAL MEETING
June 25, 2021
Memphis, Tennessee
(EXCERPTS FROM THE MORNING SESSION)

VII. President's Address

President Boyd extended his appreciation to Student Trustee Leighton Chappell and Professor Christina Vogel and welcomed new Trustee Patterson, incoming Student Trustee Lane Gutridge, and Dr. Richey, Faculty Representative to the Education, Research, and Service Committee.

President Boyd expressed his excitement for what may be a very historic meeting of the Board of Trustees with consideration of the proposed acquisition of the assets of Martin Methodist College. If approved, the University of Tennessee Southern (UT Southern) will be the first new undergraduate campus in the UT System in 50 years, as well as the first new public institution in Tennessee in 50 years.

VIII. Proposed Acquisition of Martin Methodist College

Chair Compton reviewed the history and the steps taken over the last nine months with regard to the proposed acquisition of Martin Methodist College (MMC). He noted the projected decline in the number of traditional college-aged students (based on age demographics) and the expected consolidations of higher education institutions.

At the executive committee meeting held on September 11, 2020, President Boyd presented the idea of a potential partnership with MMC, which was the subject of a non-binding letter of intent. Since then, the University administration has conducted due diligence, with the assistance of an outside consultant (Huron Consulting Group). One of the key findings of the report was the reduction in the number of high school students in Southern Middle Tennessee pursuing a college education and the potential adverse consequences to the State's Drive to 55 initiative. At a specially called meeting of the board held on December 9, 2020, the board was updated on the findings of the administrations due diligence review and tasked the administration with performing further work and analysis in four key areas. Specifically, the administration was asked to provide the board with the following:

- A market assessment regarding potential enrollment,
- A more in-depth analysis of the academic programs needed to support the vision for the campus,
- An economic model reflective of the changes needed to support the campus for long-term success, and
- A plan for stakeholder engagement.

Chair Compton stated that this follow-up information was shared with the full board and presented at the January 22, 2021, Executive Committee meeting. In February, the board was updated on Gov. Lee's budget, including recurring and non-recurring funding. Chair Compton advised that it is very difficult to receive recurring funding and that Gov. Lee and the members of the Tennessee legislature have taken significant steps in support of the proposed, new UT Southern campus.

Chair Compton, on behalf of the board, thanked President Boyd for his efforts in keeping the Board fully informed through each step of this process.

Panel Presentation and Transaction Overview

President Boyd began by sharing his vision for the UT Southern campus and the impact that it will have on the surrounding community and the State of Tennessee. He noted that the area was in desperate need of an affordable, public institution of higher education. President Boyd extended his gratitude to: (i) the board of trustees for their constructive input throughout this process, (ii) Gov. Lee for his support for rural communities and education; (iii) the state legislature for approval of the funding request; (iv) the various state agencies that have advanced this initiative; (v) the members of the teams who have worked on the project; and (vi) most importantly, to Mark La Branche, president of Martin Methodist College, for his altruistic approach and focus on the best interests of current and prospective students.

President Boyd introduced members of the senior leadership team (Linda C. Martin, vice president for Academic Affairs and Student Success; David L. Miller, senior vice president and chief financial officer; and Tiffany U. Carpenter, vice president for communications and marketing), who provided an update regarding the work that was done since the board's last meeting with state agencies, accrediting bodies and others to obtain the necessary approvals to proceed with the acquisition of the assets of Martin Methodist in order to establish a new UT campus, to be known as the University of Tennessee Southern (UT Southern). Additionally, the senior leadership team reviewed the preparation and transition plans for each of their areas, along with next steps, should the board vote to proceed. A copy of the full presentation is filed with the minutes.

Mark La Branche, president of Martin Methodist College, addressed the board. In his remarks, he reflected on the trends in higher education, which have impacted small, private, church-affiliated institutions, especially those serving in rural areas. He acknowledged the work of MMC in continuing to develop a more sustainable model. However, as the only four-year and graduate institution in the region, the demands are much greater than a small college can meet. President La Branche discussed the work of the MMC Board in being transparent prior to the pandemic, and the existential moment that arose out of the COVID-19 crisis. He shared that the MMC Board felt that it was time to become more serious about pursuing partnerships, collaborations and even mergers.

He reflected that the action before the two boards is the culmination of more than a year's worth of planning. The prospective establishment of UT Southern campus, as the fourth undergraduate institution in the UT System, will rest on the foundation of more than 151 years of mission. Based on the stewardship of the MMC Board and the dutiful care of the faculty and staff, MMC comes to this point not in a deficit, but poised for great growth. He believes that the proposed acquisition is not about what exists now, but rather about a tremendous promise for the future. He recognized the debt owed to the Methodist movement, which considers growing knowledge a divine pursuit and one that should be available for all. He hopes that the actions before the boards will aid in the pursuit of that mission. President La Branche spoke of the fierce headwinds that MMC has battled over the years, and how it feels good to have some wind at their back. He also quoted the French poet Victor Hugo in saying that "nothing is more powerful than an idea whose time has come."

President La Branche spoke of his leadership team's commitment to pursuing this initiative, even if it meant stepping aside for the sake of the mission. He extended his gratitude to both boards of trustees, to President Randy Boyd for thinking outside the box and for his personal, financial commitment to ensuring the resources necessary, to the elected officials who were willing to take on something of this magnitude during the biggest health crises in nearly 100 years and to the leadership teams of both organizations for their tireless efforts.

President La Branche closed his remarks by stating that it will be an honor and privilege to serve the university and assist it in fulfilling its promise as a great land grant university system. He then shared some of the immediate results in enrollment and retention, and his belief that, moving forward, the campus will more than exceed the projections. His remarks were met with applause.

Review of the Proposed Agreements and Questions and Comments

Mr. Stinnett reviewed the following items: (i) the overall structure of the proposed asset acquisition, (ii) key provisions of the Asset Transfer and Transition Agreement and other related documents and (iii) the approvals received and the remaining action items.

Chair Compton thanked the presenters and opened the floor to the trustees for questions and comments. The trustees engaged in a robust discussion of the merits of the proposed acquisition in general and, in particular, with respect to the university's land grant mission, the UT System Strategic Plan, and the needs of the region and the state of Tennessee.

The trustees agreed that the acquisition of the assets of MMC and establishment of UT Southern would be a win for students, the employees and the citizens of the state. Trustee Hatcher also noted that the acquisition was strongly based in the mission of a land grant university and aligned with Gov. Lee's Rural Initiative. Growth in university enrollment is a stated objective of the UT System Strategic Plan. From a stakeholders' perspective, the acquisition includes strong local community support (i.e., business leaders and others closely connected to MMC). Moreover, the trustees expressed their excitement about the alignment of the missions of the two institutions and the university's opportunity to make a meaningful difference in the lives of individuals who live in the area.

Moving forward with the implementation, the trustees encouraged the teams to abandon the differences that do not matter, but to embrace items that are uniquely important. The trustees also expressed their appreciation for the hard work demonstrated by the teams of both institutions, acknowledging the complexities associated with mergers/acquisitions.

Approvals

Asset Transfer and Transition Agreement

Following the presentation by Mr. Stinnett, Chair Compton called for a motion to approve the Asset Transfer and Transition Agreement, as presented in Tab 3.2 of the meeting materials. Upon motion duly made and seconded, the board approved Resolution 028-2021, by unanimous roll call vote.

Appointment and Compensation of Chancellor

President Boyd recommended the appointment of Mark La Branche as the inaugural chancellor of the University of Tennessee Southern, based on the terms and compensation presented to the board (Tab 3.3). Upon motion duly made and seconded, the board approved Resolution 029-2021 by unanimous roll call vote. Chair Compton extended the board's congratulations to Chancellor La Branche. Chancellor La Branche thanked his wife, Mona, for her support throughout this process.

Academic Programs

Dr. Martin provided a brief overview of the work done to ensure that UT Southern's academic programs are aligned and consistent with the policies set forth by the Tennessee

Higher Education Commission (THEC). The academic programs for UT Southern were provided under Tab 3.4 of the meeting materials circulated in advance of the meeting. Upon motion duly made and seconded, the board approved Resolution 030-2021 by unanimous roll call vote.

President La Branche's remarks to the UT Board of Trustees–June 25, 2021

What our boards will vote on today is the culmination of more than a year of preparation and planning. It is important to note that the establishment of the University of Tennessee Southern as the fourth undergraduate campus of the University of Tennessee System rests upon the strong foundation of 151 years of mission.

Due to the dutiful stewardship of the Martin Methodist Trustees and the excellent care of the Martin Methodist staff and faculty, we come to this moment not at a deficit but poised for great growth.

We are indebted to the Methodist movement that considered growing in knowledge a divine pursuit, a pursuit that should be available to all. It is this priority that established our foundation and mission.

What we do today will aid the pursuit of that mission in a phenomenal way. You see, we have acquired each other, and the implications will reverberate for another 151 years.

Our mission has often braved fierce headwinds over these many years, and it is so good to feel the wind at our back.

Victor Hugo the French poet said "Nothing is more powerful than an idea whose time has come."

This process that began as an idea was so compelling to the Martin Methodist leadership team that we committed ourselves to do whatever it took to accomplish this, even if it meant stepping aside.

We come to this day filled with gratitude. We are grateful that we will take these next steps with you.

We also recognize the extraordinary leadership of the Martin Methodist College an UT System Boards of Trustees.

Our trustees have engaged at a level that is rare but critically important. The UT System BOT lived out what has already been recognized by the Association of Governing Boards in the awarding of the Nason Award, awarded to higher education governing boards that demonstrate exceptional leadership and initiative.

We are grateful for our President Randy Boyd whose energy, passion and vision are inspiring, and without which we would not be at this historic juncture today.

We are grateful for the UT System staff, chancellors, and their teams. They have all been extremely hospitable and a delight to work with.

Last, but not least, we are grateful for our elected leadership, who positioned the state of Tennessee to accomplish this during the biggest health crisis in more than 100 years. Generations will look back and marvel at what is taking place.

Once again, it is an honor and privilege serve with you to fulfill the promise of this great land grant state university.

Board Resolution from June 25, 2021

University of Tennessee
Board of Trustees
Resolution 028-2021
Acquisition of Martin Methodist College

WHEREAS, the rates of postsecondary attainment in the Southern Middle Tennessee region significantly lag the state's overall rate as well as the target of 55% set out in Tennessee's Drive to 55 campaign;

WHEREAS, there is evidence that indicates an unmet labor need for educated workers in the region as well as the state more broadly;

WHEREAS, increasing access to quality, affordable, public education through an expanded presence of the University of Tennessee ("University") in this part of the state may be an effective means of improving the state's college-going rate and addressing unmet labor need;

WHEREAS, Martin Methodist College ("MMC"), founded in 1870, is a private, liberal arts, four-year college located in Pulaski, Tennessee;

WHEREAS, through the acquisition of substantially all of the assets of MMC, the University would have the opportunity to establish a new University campus in Giles County that would serve prospective students in the southern middle region of Tennessee, an area that has been underserved;

WHEREAS such action would be consistent with the University's land-grant designation and its mission of delivering education, discovery, outreach and public service that contributes to the economic, social and environmental well-being of all Tennesseans; and

WHEREAS, the University officers have sought and obtained the necessary authorizations of the Tennessee General Assembly, acting through legislation, resolution or appropriations, to acquire substantially all of the assets of MMC;

NOW, THEREFORE, BE IT RESOLVED AS FOLLOWS:

Subject to receipt of any other required governmental approvals, the proper University officers are hereby authorized to execute and deliver the Asset Transfer and Transition Agreement (the "Agreement"), which shall be substantially in the form attached hereto as Attachment A.

As contemplated within the Agreement, the Board of Trustees hereby approves the establishment of a new University campus, to be known as "the University of Tennessee Southern."

As contemplated within the Agreement, the Board of Trustees hereby approves the award of tenure to the faculty members identified in the Agreement.

The proper officers of the University be and hereby are authorized to take any and all such actions as may be required or which they may deem necessary or appropriate in order to complete the acquisition.

Adopted this 25th day of June, 2021.

Key Steps and Approvals in the Acquisition Process

DATE	STEP/APPROVAL	DESCRIPTION
September 2020	Letter of Intent	MMC and UT officials signed a nonbinding letter of intent on Sept. 11, 2020.
September 2020	Stakeholder engagement	MMC and UT presidents begin a series of events—town halls, meetings, discussions, videos, surveys, focus groups—to discuss the potential acquisition, answer questions, listen to concerns, and seek input and ideas.
Fall 2020	Due diligence process	UT partnered with Huron Consulting to conduct strategic, market, financial and operational due diligence. Report issued Dec. 1, 2020.
September–October 2020	Facilities condition assessment	Bureau Veritas, retained by UT, performed the assessment and issued its findings in October.
December 2020	UT Board of Trustees action	The UT Board authorized UT leaders to continue negotiations and seek necessary approvals in special meeting on Dec. 9, 2020.
December 2020	MMC Board of Trustees action	The MMC Board approved the potential acquisition of Martin Methodist by the UT System in a meeting on Dec. 9, 2020.
December 2020	Trustees of the Tennessee Conference of the United Methodist Church	The trustees approved the release of the assets of MMC in a specially called meeting on Dec. 9, 2020, contingent upon the approval of the full annual conference expected in June 2021.

DATE	STEP/APPROVAL	DESCRIPTION
December 2020	Multiple statements of support issued	Government officials and other leaders from the Southern Middle Tennessee region and beyond express support for the acquisition.
January 2021	UT Board of Trustees Executive Committee meeting	The committee was updated on UT officials' analysis of key issues raised in the December board meeting. Report issued Jan. 15, 2021.
February 2021	Governor's budget proposal released	Gov. Bill Lee's proposed budget revealed in his Feb. 8, 2021, State of the State Address included a request for $5.1 million recurring/$1 million nonrecurring for the acquisition and startup costs.
February 2021	Integration planning and negotiation of asset transfer agreement begins	Teams of UT and MMC officials begin planning for the potential integration after notice of governor's funding request, including drafting the asset transfer agreement.
February 2021	Survey to MMC stakeholders	UT Marketing and Communications staff conducted surveys with various MMC stakeholders to obtain input on team name, mascot and school colors.
March 2021	Formal resolutions in favor of the acquisition issued.	Officials throughout the Southern Middle Tennessee region—city/county mayors, chambers of commerce leaders and economic development officials—took the extraordinary step of passing formal resolutions in favor of the acquisition.
March 2021	MMC submits Substantive Change Prospectus to regional accreditor, SACSCOC	The prospectus concerned the potential transfer of ownership of MMC to UT, as required by the Southern Association of Colleges and Schools Commission on Colleges to maintain accreditation.
April 2021	TN General Assembly passes FY21-22 budget	The budget, approved on April 29, 2021, included the governor's requested recurring and nonrecurring funding for the acquisition.

DATE	STEP/APPROVAL	DESCRIPTION
May 2021	Office of Attorney General "No Action" Letter	The Public Interest Division of the attorney general's office, which oversees nonprofits, reviewed the proposed asset transfer agreement and declined to take action (thereby consenting).
June 2021	Conference of the United Methodist Church approval	On June 10, 2021, the Tennessee Annual Conference of the United Methodist Church approved a resolution allowing Martin Methodist College to join the UT System.
June 2021	TSSBA approval	Approval for UT to obtain a commercial loan to settle MMC debt to the USDA at a June 15, 2021, Tennessee State School Bond Authority meeting.
June 2021	SACSCOC Board	Approval of the MMC prospectus regarding a change in ownership by end of June 15–17, 2021, board meeting.
June 2021	UT Board of Trustees	Approval of asset transfer agreement and related items at the June 25, 2021, meeting.
June 2021	MMC Board of Trustees	Approval of asset transfer agreement and related items at the June 25, 2021, meeting.
June 2021	State Building Commission	Approval of the MMC property acquisition at the June 28 SBC Executive Committee meeting.
June 2021	Asset transfer agreement	Executed by UT and MMC officials.
July 2021	Acquisition	July 1, 2021, effective date